HOW TO STOP PEOPLE PLEASING AND BE YOURSELF

Breaking the Chains of Approval— Saying "No" Without Guilt and Unleashing Your True Self by Mastering the Art of Authentic Living

Delmar Bolton

TABLE OF CONTENT

Introduction

Larry was a diligent worker at the bustling poultry farm on the outskirts of town. His days were filled with the rhythmic clucking of hens and the mundane duties required preserving the farm's feathery occupants' well-being. Larry had a strong work ethic and was noted for his unrelenting dedication to his duties.

Larry, on the other hand, was engaged in a hidden struggle. He was strongly aware that the quality of the bird meals was deteriorating. The components weren't up to Larry's customary standards, and he was concerned about the poultry's health. Larry hesitated to express his concerns despite his awareness. He was a people-pleaser at heart, always seeking unity and the approval of his superiors.

Larry's internal struggle reached a boiling point when he watched the unloading of a cargo of inferior feed. He knew he couldn't keep quiet any longer, but he was afraid of upsetting his employer. Larry's eagerness to please everyone, especially those in charge, exceeded his concern for the birds' well-being.

Trouble was brewing in the background. Larry carried on with his responsibilities, feeding the tainted meal to the fowl, expecting that the matter would resolve itself. Unfortunately, it didn't take long for customers to start complaining. The tainted feed had resulted in a drop in egg quality, and the farm's once-thriving reputation began to dwindle.

Larry was surprised to learn that he was the first to face the repercussions. In quest of a scapegoat, the farm's administration chose Larry as the sacrificial lamb. The failure of the tainted feed eclipsed his years of hard work and effort. Larry, the hardworking employee who went above and beyond to please everyone, was let go unexpectedly.

Larry had to swallow the bitter pill of being fired despite his best efforts to keep everyone pleased. He understood the cost of putting others' happiness ahead of his values. Larry eventually realized that true dedication entails sticking up for what is right, even if it means upsetting people in control.

Larry departed the chicken farm with the hard-earned knowledge that pleasing everyone at the expense of integrity is a dangerous route to take. His adventure continued, but this time he was determined to put doing the right thing over seeking continual acceptance.

Defining People-Pleasing

People-pleasing is a prevalent thread in the complicated mosaic of human interactions, often woven into the fabric of our daily lives. To grasp the essence of people-pleasing, we must first define it and then go into the numerous layers that constitute this complicated social phenomenon.

Unmasking People-Pleasing

At its foundation, people-pleasing is the compulsive drive to seek approval and affirmation from others by putting their wants and aspirations over one's own. It takes the form of a range of behaviors intended at preserving harmony, avoiding confrontation, and winning acceptance. This deeply ingrained tendency is frequently motivated by a genuine desire for connection and positive reinforcement.

Individuals trapped in the web of people-pleasing may find themselves saying "yes" to obligations they would rather decline or hiding their genuine ideas in order to conform to others' perceived expectations. The core of people-pleasing is sacrificing one's authenticity in order to gain external favor.

The Urge to Please

People-pleasing is motivated by a strong desire to be liked and accepted. Individuals that engage in people-pleasing habits are frequently on the lookout for external validation, fearing rejection or condemnation. This desire to please can emerge in a variety of settings, ranging from personal relationships to the workplace, where the demand for approval drives decision-making.

The origins of the desire to please are frequently found in early social conditioning, where individuals learn that adhering to societal standards results in positive reinforcement. This conditioning develops over time into a subconscious desire for approval, even at the price of one's real self. Fear of disappointing others becomes an effective motivator, altering behavior and decision-making.

Approval Social Dynamics

Understanding people-pleasing necessitates a look at the societal dynamics that contribute to its popularity. Individuals are pressured to conform by society's dense network of conventions and expectations. Fear of being an anomaly or receiving criticism feeds the need to please others, resulting in a delicate dance between personal authenticity and society norms.

The social dynamics of approbation include the impression of oneself as seen by others. People-pleasers frequently focus their self-worth on external validation, establishing a cycle of reliance on others' opinions and approval. This external focus of validation can lead to a state of continual worry as individuals traverse the perilous terrain of meeting the expectations of others.

The Control Illusion

People-pleasers frequently assume that by matching others' expectations, they can exert influence over the dynamics of their relationships and situations. To negotiate the ambiguities of social interactions, the illusion of control becomes a coping tool. Individuals may, however, sacrifice their authenticity in the search of outward harmony, unknowingly forsaking their own wants and ideals.

This misconception extends beyond interpersonal connections and into the workplace. People-pleasers may find themselves taking on excessive workloads, agreeing to tasks outside of their job specifications, and being hesitant to express limits in order to control perceptions and preserve a positive image.

Navigating the Gray Areas

People-pleasing is difficult to define because it encompasses a wide range of behaviors. It is critical to discern between healthy social adaptability and an unhealthy desire to please. While accommodating others is a natural part of social dynamics, it becomes problematic when it comes at the expense of one's own well-being and authenticity.

Navigating the murky waters of people-pleasing necessitates introspection and a strong awareness of one's own motivations. Flexible social interactions are necessary for healthy adaptability, but when behaviors are motivated by fear, anxiety, or an insatiable need for acceptance, it's an indication that the line has been crossed into people-pleasing zone.

Consequences of People-Pleasing

As we seek a full knowledge of people-pleasing, it is critical to shine light on the consequences that frequently accompany this well-meaning but mistaken activity. As the cycle continues, the toll on one's mental and emotional well-being becomes more obvious.

The constant search for external validation can result in increased tension, anxiety, and a sense of everlasting discontent. People-pleasers may become trapped in a cycle of over commitment, burning out as they attempt to meet the ever-increasing expectations of others around them. Another casualty is the erosion of self-esteem, as the individual is more defined by the judgments of others rather than an actual sense of self-worth.

Liberation from People-Pleasing

The path to liberation from the chains of people-pleasing is both liberating and transforming. It all starts with self-awareness, a fearless acknowledgement of the pattern's presence, and a will to change. Recognizing that the need to please stems from a fear of rejection is a critical first step.

Breaking free entails developing a healthy sense of self-worth that is independent of external affirmation. Redefining one's priorities, learning to create and communicate limits, and embracing the power of saying "no" when necessary are all part of the process. People-pleasing emancipation is regaining authenticity and cultivating relationships based on mutual respect rather than a continuous hunt for acceptance.

Embracing Authenticity

The journey toward accepting authenticity is at the heart of understanding people-pleasing. Authenticity entails acting in accordance with one's actual principles and ideas, even if it means diverging from society norms. It is a significant transition from seeking approval to living in accordance with one's genuine self.

Adopting sincerity is a life-changing experience. It entails self-reflection, reevaluating priorities, and having the courage to communicate one's thoughts and feelings authentically. Individuals discover a sense of empowerment and pleasure that exceeds the fleeting gratification of external affirmation when they peel back the layers of people-pleasing.

Striking a Balance

While breaking away from people-pleasing is an admirable goal, it is critical to remember that effective social relationships require some respect for others. The secret to long-term partnerships is to strike a balance between appeasing others and remaining authentic. This equilibrium allows for true interaction without jeopardizing personal well-being.

Looking Ahead

People-pleasing requires a multifaceted investigation into the subtle interplay of societal dynamics, personal motivations, and the pursuit for authenticity. We shall explore deeper into the features, implications, and options for release from the pervasive grasp of people-pleasing as we progress through the chapters. The path toward authenticity is a never-ending adventure, and the insights obtained in these pages will serve as a guide for anyone seeking a truer and fulfilling living.

Setting the Stage for Self-Discovery

Self-discovery serves as the music that moves us ahead in the complicated dance of life, guiding us through the steps of knowing who we are at our core. Setting the environment for self-discovery is critical before going on the process of breaking free from people-pleasing. This chapter delves into the basic aspects and factors that serve as the foundation for an authentic self-exploration.

The Awareness Prelude

The process of self-discovery begins with a profound sense of awareness—the conscious recognition of one's thoughts, emotions, and behaviors. It entails removing layers of indoctrination and societal expectations to expose the true self beneath. The stage is prepared for awareness by asking people to explore fundamental questions about their beliefs, desires, and the motivations that drive their actions.

Awareness becomes a beacon in the setting of people-pleasing, illuminating the habits and tendencies that undermine personal authenticity. Individuals must become aware of the subtle indicators and feelings that accompany their people-pleasing acts to create an environment conducive to self-reflection.

Cultivating Curiosity

A curious spirit becomes the leading force in the voyage of self-discovery. Curiosity is developed by approaching oneself with an open mind, free of judgment. It's about asking yourself not just "What do I do?" but also "Why do I do it?" and "How does it align with my true self?" People that cultivate curiosity create an environment for learning, helping them to uncover the rationales behind their behaviors as well as the fundamental ideas that may be impacting their behavior.

Curiosity becomes a tool for understanding the intricate network of approval-seeking activities in the setting of people-pleasing. It encourages people to investigate the sources of their desire to please, such as childhood experiences, cultural expectations, or a deep-seated fear of rejection.

The Role of Introspection

Introspection is required for self-discovery—a deliberate and sincere investigation of one's ideas, feelings, and motivations. It's an introspective journey led by the goal of profoundly understanding oneself. Introspection entails carving out time in solitude to reflect on past events, recognize patterns of conduct, and identify the tiny whispers of the inner self.

Introspection becomes a valuable tool for unraveling the layers of conditioned responses for those bound in the web of people-pleasing. It encourages people to reflect on times when they strayed from their true selves to please others. They can begin to detect the patterns and triggers that lead to people-pleasing actions through introspection.

Creating Space for Authenticity

Setting the setting for self-discovery entails creating an environment in which authenticity can bloom. This entails clearing up the mental and emotional environment, eliminating the masks worn for cultural acceptability, and allowing the actual self to shine. Making room for authenticity involves a commitment to being honest with oneself and with others.

Creating room for authenticity in the context of people-pleasing entails admitting the discomfort that may emerge when facing the potential of enforcing boundaries or expressing true opinions. It is about acknowledging that honesty while challenging existing standards, is necessary for a fuller and true existence.

Embracing Vulnerability

The path to self-discovery is fraught with danger. It takes bravery to confront areas of oneself that are uncomfortable or unknown. Accepting faults, addressing worries of judgment, and allowing oneself to be seen truthfully are all part of embracing vulnerability.

Embracing vulnerability becomes a catalyst for change for those who are engaged in people-pleasing. It entails acknowledging the difficulty associated with setting boundaries and the fear of disappointing people. Individuals can build stronger connections with themselves and others through vulnerability, laying the framework for a more honest and satisfying existence.

The Art of Mindfulness

Mindfulness is a helpful companion on the journey of self-discovery. Being fully present in the moment entails examining thoughts and emotions without judgment and cultivating a heightened awareness of the present experience. Mindfulness encourages people to separate themselves from automatic reactions, making room for thoughtful and real answers.

Mindfulness becomes a technique for breaking out from reactive tendencies in the setting of people-pleasing. It invites people to pause, reflect on their intentions, and consider alternate, more authentic replies. Individuals who practice mindfulness can handle the difficulties of social interactions with greater clarity and intention.

Setting Intentions for Growth

Setting growth intentions is the climax of laying the groundwork for self-discovery. This phase is committing to an ongoing process of discovering oneself, embracing authenticity, and fostering a more authentic manner of engaging with the world. Setting intentions serves as a road map for the trip ahead, leading individuals through the inevitable trials and tribulations of self-discovery.

Setting growth goals entails a commitment to emphasizing authenticity over external validation for those attempting to overcome people-pleasing habits. It is about knowing that self-discovery is a journey, not a destination and that it is distinguished by self-reflection, learning, and the persistent pursuit of a more authentic existence.

Overcoming Obstacles

Setting the stage for self-discovery is fraught with difficulties. The trip may reveal difficult realities, challenge long-held beliefs, and necessitate confronting previously concealed portions of oneself. Navigating these difficulties necessitates resilience, self-compassion, and a willingness to learn.

Individuals may experience obstacles from both internal and external factors when it comes to people-pleasing. Fear of offending others, the discomfort of enforcing limits, and the uncertainty of navigating novel social dynamics can all cause difficulties. Navigating these difficulties necessitates a firm commitment to the ideals of self-discovery as well as a realization that progress frequently develops from difficulty.

Seeking Support

Going on a self-discovery journey is not a solitary undertaking. Seeking advice and encouragement from trusted friends, family members, or professionals can be quite beneficial. Sharing one's experiences, ideas, and challenges with others develops a sense of connection and emphasizes the value of community on the route to authenticity.

Seeking support for those navigating the complexity of people-pleasing entails reaching out to others who can offer understanding, empathy, and critical critique. Seeking assistance, whether through casual talks with trusted friends or formal advice from mental health specialists, improves the resilience and efficacy of the self-discovery process.

Cultivating Patience

Self-discovery is a journey that takes its own time. Patience becomes a crucial characteristic, allowing people to accept the ebb and flow of the process. Patience entails accepting that the journey to self-discovery is not a straight line, with peaks of understanding, plateaus of reflection, and valleys of uncertainty.

Patience is especially crucial when it comes to pleasing others. It's about accepting that breaking free from old behaviors takes time and involves compassion for both accomplishments and setbacks. Patience becomes an ally, sustaining the momentum of self-discovery and encouraging individuals to continue in the face of adversity.

This comprehensive guide prepares the way for the transformative voyage of self-discovery, which is required before breaking free from the shackles of people-pleasing. The following chapters will dive into the features of people-pleasing, as well as its consequences.

CHAPTER TWO

The Allure of People-Pleasing

The appeal of people-pleasing develops as a mesmerizing rhythm in the complicated dance of social interaction, enticing individuals to negotiate the delicate steps of approval-seeking. To understand the complexities of people-pleasing, we must first unravel the appeal that attracts people to this sophisticated dance and then investigate the underlying causes that make it such a common pattern in human behavior.

The Magnetic Urge

A magnetic urge—an inner want to be liked, accepted, and validated by others around us—is at the heart of the attractiveness of people-pleasing. This motivating drive frequently begins in childhood, when cultural standards and household expectations provide the framework for seeking praise. The temptation of pleasing others stems from the assumption that by satisfying others' expectations, one might gain a sense of belonging while avoiding the discomfort of rejection.

The Social Currency of Approval

Approval serves as a social currency, a sort of interpersonal transaction that feeds the appeal of pleasing others. In a world where connections are highly valued, approval becomes a valuable commodity. The temptation stems from the belief that acquiring this currency will result in smoother interactions, improved relationships, and a greater sense of self-worth.

Individuals drawn to the appeal of people-pleasing frequently engage in acts designed to gain favor. The allure rests in the notion that these activities will earn good recognition and enhance a sense of social value, whether through agreeing with others, avoiding conflicts, or taking on excessive obligations.

Fear of Disapproval

Fear of disapproval is a crucial aspect of the appeal of people-pleasing—a potent incentive that encourages individuals to adhere to cultural norms. This dread, which stems from the human need for social connection, pushes people to value the preferences of others over their honest expressions. When people view rejection as a danger to their sense of belonging and self-esteem, the allure of people-pleasing increases.

Fear of rejection, which frequently stems from early experiences with conditional love or acceptance, becomes a driving force in the allure of people-pleasing. Individuals are propelled into a never-ending loop of seeking approval, even at the expense of their own needs and principles, to avoid disagreement and preserve a positive image.

Conditional Self-Worth

The temptation of pleasing others is inextricably linked to a conditional sense of self-worth. Individuals who succumb to this attraction frequently get their worth from external validation rather than an innate awareness of their worth. The allure is in the notion that pleasing others will provide a stable foundation of self-worth based on external affirmations.

People-pleasers' conditional self-worth generates a never-ending loop of seeking approval. The allure derives from the concept that pleasing others provides a brief boost to one's self-esteem, reinforcing the notion that external validation is the major source of personal value.

The Illusion of Control

The sense of control it affords in managing social situations is one of the most appealing aspects of people-pleasing. The assumption that one can change the dynamics of relationships by accommodating others becomes a seductive lure. The allure stems from the belief that by pleasing others, individuals can form favorable perceptions, prevent conflicts, and maintain a sense of peace in their social spheres.

The appearance of control becomes enticing in people-pleasing, obscuring the underlying worries and insecurities that drive such activities. The appeal of being the architect of happy connections while avoiding potential rejection enhances people-pleasing's compulsive character.

Social Norms and Expectations

The temptation of pleasing others is inextricably linked to society expectations and conventions. Individuals are socialized from a young age to comply with specific actions and adhere to cultural standards of politeness and agreeability. The allure is in the ease of conforming to these expectations, while deviating may result in social ostracism.

As individuals seek to fit into established patterns, the influence of society's expectations becomes a powerful force, defining the appeal of people-pleasing. The allure is propelled by the fear of standing out or suffering criticism, prompting individuals to value conformity over real expression.

Short-Term Gratification

The allure of pleasing others is often enhanced by the immediate enjoyment it delivers. The instant rewards of approbation, praise, and pleasant relationships set in motion a feedback loop. The attractiveness of people-pleasing rests in the immediate and concrete benefits it provides, even if these benefits are fleeting and do not lead to long-term contentment.

Individuals enamored with the attraction of pleasing others may find temporary joy in the positive reactions of others. The fascination is maintained by the fleeting sense of accomplishment and affirmation, which fosters a habit that becomes firmly ingrained in the search of quick gratification.

Conflict Avoidance

The capacity to avoid conflict and confrontation is one of the most enticing aspects of people-pleasing. The allure is in avoiding awkward or challenging conversations, which allows people to preserve an appearance of calm and harmony. Fear of disagreement or rejection becomes a potent incentive, boosting the appeal of pleasing others behaviors.

Individuals emphasize maintaining positive relationships over expressing their real thoughts and feelings, which contributes to the appeal of people-pleasing. Conflict avoidance becomes a habit, strengthening the appeal of people-pleasing in interpersonal dynamics.

Social Comparison

The appeal of pleasing others is frequently fostered by social comparison—the desire to judge one's worth based on the apparent triumphs and approvals of others. The allure stems from the need to live up to society's standards and benchmarks, prompting individuals to engage in people-pleasing actions to conform to perceived norms of success and popularity.

As individuals attempt to meet or exceed their peers' perceived successes, social comparison becomes a driving force in the appeal of people-pleasing. Fear of falling short or being unfairly compared drives people-pleasers to seek acceptance all the time, reinforcing the allure of comparison as a yardstick for self-worth.

The Role of Early Conditioning

The temptation to please others is inextricably linked to early conditioning—the process by which individuals adopt behavioral patterns and coping mechanisms during their formative years. The allure derives from the familiarity and perceived safety of childhood actions, where seeking approval may have been a means of ensuring affection, attention, or safety.

Early training contributes significantly to the appeal of people-pleasing by influencing individuals' reactions to social cues. The behaviors developed in childhood linger into adulthood, establishing the foundation of the allure as people continue to seek the validation and praise that were so important in their childhood.

This comprehensive exploration unravels the multifaceted allure of people-pleasing, shedding light on the intricate motivations that draw individuals into this intricate dance of approval-seeking. The following chapters will go into greater detail about the features, consequences, and tactics for breaking free from the pull of people-pleasing, providing insights into a more authentic and meaningful manner of navigating social interactions.

Understanding the Urge to Please

The need to please emerges as a motivating force that impacts our behaviors, decisions, and relationships in the complex landscape of human interaction. The second chapter goes into the complexities of comprehending the need to please, investigating the underlying motivations, psychological mechanisms, and societal influences that contribute to this widespread characteristic of human conduct.

The Evolutionary Roots

Understanding the need to please necessitates a voyage into our evolutionary past when social relationships and group dynamics were critical to existence. The need to please stems from an underlying desire for social connection and cooperation. Individuals who were welcomed and valued by the group had a better chance of survival and reproduction in primitive cultures. This evolutionary history contributes to the profound desire to please to gain social approval and support.

The Neurobiology of Pleasure

The desire to please is neurobiologically tied to the brain's reward system. Acts of pleasing others engage pleasure and reinforcement areas of the brain, releasing chemicals like dopamine that provide a sensation of contentment and well-being. This neurological response strengthens the need to please, establishing a loop in which people seek the pleasurable benefits of social approval.

Understanding the physiology of pleasure helps to explain why the desire to please becomes so engrained in human behavior. The reward system of the brain becomes a driving force, urging people to engage in behaviors that result in positive social outcomes.

Social Conditioning and Upbringing

Social conditioning and upbringing have a huge influence on the desire to please. Individuals are taught societal conventions, manners, and the necessity of pleasing others from an early age. Positive reinforcement for pleasing acts and negative consequences for displeasing actions all help to shape the desire to please as a learned behavior.

Understanding the function of social conditioning and upbringing in unraveling the desire to please is critical. Early experiences affect behavior patterns, laying the groundwork for seeking approval and avoiding criticism as a strategy for gaining love, attention, and validation.

Fear of Rejection and Disapproval

Fear of rejection and disapproval is a key component of the desire to please. Humans are social creatures by nature, and the dread of being cast out or socially ostracized elicits a strong emotional response. The need to please emerges as a protective mechanism to reduce the perceived threat of rejection, so assuring social inclusion and acceptability.

Understanding the fear of rejection as a motivator for the desire to please sheds light on the emotional basis of this conduct. The fear of being judged becomes a potent motivator, influencing decision-making and interpersonal interactions.

Low Self-Esteem and Insecurity

The need to please is frequently accompanied by low self-esteem and insecurity. Individuals who have a low sense of self-worth may seek external affirmation to help them maintain their fragile self-image. To compensate for emotions of inadequacy and self-doubt, the need to please becomes a compensatory mechanism.

Understanding the relationship between poor self-esteem and the need to please reveals the psychological intricacies at work. The desire for external approval becomes a technique to momentarily assuage internal concerns, creating a cycle in which individuals seek validation from others on an ongoing basis.

Societal Expectations and Norms

The desire to please is heavily influenced by societal expectations and standards. Individuals are taught from a young age to conform to cultural ideals of civility, agreeability, and social peace. The desire to please stems from a desire to meet these expectations to avoid the discomfort of departing from established norms.

Understanding the influence of societal standards highlights the external influences that contribute to the desire to please. Individuals emphasize conformity above true expression out of fear of sticking out or suffering judgment.

Learned Behaviors and Reinforcement

The desire to please is frequently the product of acquired actions that are reinforced by positive outcomes. Individuals who receive praise, awards, or acknowledgment for pleasing acts develop similar behaviors as techniques for gaining approval. The desire to please becomes a habitual response over time, encouraged by the favorable outcomes associated with such acts.

Understanding the role of learnt behaviors and reinforcement in the development and maintenance of the want to please throws light on the development and maintenance of the desire to please. To break out from this cycle, you must make a conscious effort to unlearn entrenched patterns and build new, real ways of connecting.

Coping Mechanism for Anxiety

The desire to please can be used to cope with anxiety and social discomfort. Anxious individuals may engage in pleasing activities to reduce their fear of judgment or criticism. The temporary alleviation from worry encourages the need to please, resulting in a vicious circle of behavior geared at coping with emotional suffering.

Understanding the desire to please as a coping technique highlights the importance of dealing with underlying worries. Breaking free from the desire to please necessitates the development of better coping methods as well as the development of resilience in the face of social uncertainties.

The Role of Empathy and Compassion

While the desire to please is often motivated by self-preservation, it can also be motivated by real empathy and compassion. Individuals may experience genuine concern for the well-being and pleasure of others, which motivates them to engage in appealing activities. Understanding the good parts of the desire to please fosters a sophisticated worldview that recognizes the possibility of genuine, loving interactions.

Recognizing the need for empathy and compassion provides a more balanced perspective on the desire to please. It enables people to distinguish between real, other-oriented goals and a compulsive need for approbation.

Cultural Influences

The manifestation of the desire to please is shaped by cultural factors, with different communities placing varying degrees of emphasis on communal harmony, individual expression, and conformity. The need to please may be stronger in collectivist cultures, where group cohesion is valued. Individualistic societies encourage human autonomy, therefore the desire to please may emerge differently.

Understanding the role of cultural factors broadens one's understanding of the desire to please. It emphasizes the variety of this behavior across different socioeconomic situations and emphasizes the significance of taking cultural variations into account when addressing the desire to please.

This in-depth examination of Chapter two dives into the many facets of comprehending the need to please, providing insights into the evolutionary, psychological, and sociological elements that contribute to this complex human phenomenon. The following chapters will delve more into the features of the need to please, its emotional and mental consequences, and solutions for navigating and transcending this widespread pattern in human behavior.

The Social Dynamics of Approval

The dynamics of approbation play a crucial part in the complicated tapestry of human interactions, influencing behavior, decisions, and self-perception. The second chapter delves deeper into the intricate interplay of social dynamics surrounding approval, delving into the nuanced interactions, societal conventions, and psychological mechanisms that determine the desire for acceptance.

Social Exchange Theory

The Social transaction Theory, a paradigm that portrays social interactions as a sort of transaction in which individuals attempt to maximize rewards and minimize costs, is at the heart of the social dynamics of approbation. Individuals engage in behaviors geared at getting positive feedback while limiting the danger of rejection in this situation, making approval a valued social currency.

Understanding Social Exchange Theory illuminates the transactional character of approval relations. Individuals negotiate social encounters with a deep awareness of the potential benefits and costs of obtaining approval, which contributes to the complicated mathematics that defines conduct.

Reciprocity and Social Obligations

Reciprocity is a crucial notion in the approval social dynamics. Positive deeds should be rewarded with positive actions, and vice versa. The desire to please is fueled by the expectation of reciprocity, as individuals engage in activities that are likely to elicit acceptance in return.

The social dynamics of acceptance are inextricably linked to feelings of social obligation. Individuals feel obligated to reciprocate approval to preserve social connections in balance. This dynamic reinforces the social network's constant loop of seeking and providing approval.

Expectations and Norms

The social dynamics of acceptance are heavily influenced by societal norms and expectations. Cultures define acceptable behavior, setting the bounds within which people seek approval. Adherence to cultural standards becomes a measure of social skill, impacting the decisions people make in their quest for acceptance.

Understanding the impact of norms and expectations sheds light on the social scripts that people follow in their pursuit of approval. Deviation from these scripts may result in acceptance being withdrawn, reinforcing conformity to established societal standards.

Group Identity and Conformity

The social dynamics of acceptance also affect group conformity and identity. Humans have an innate desire to belong, and group participation frequently serves as a source of approbation and affirmation. Individuals may conform to group norms and behaviors to gain praise from their peers and maintain their sense of group identification.

The intersection between group conformity and approval dynamics highlights the complexities of social relationships. Individuals who seek approval may be influenced to adopt group values, even if they vary from their genuine selves.

Status and Social Comparison

The social dynamics of approval are inextricably tied to social comparison, a widespread component of human psychology. Individuals frequently assess their value and achievement in comparison to others, seeking acceptance by meeting or exceeding accepted societal criteria. As individuals participate in actions aimed at outperforming their peers, the quest for status becomes a driving factor.

Understanding the role of social comparison in approval dynamics provides insights into the competitive character of approval dynamics. The fear of falling short or being unfairly compared drives people to constantly seek approval, contributing to the never-ending cycle of comparison.

Power Dynamics and Authority

Power dynamics and authority also have an impact on the social dynamics of approval. Individuals in positions of power or authority have the authority to provide or deny permission, influencing the behavior of others seeking validation. The fear of upsetting authority figures can drive people to comply with expectations, even if it means sacrificing their principles.

Understanding power dynamics reveals the asymmetry of approval interactions. When seeking validation from persons with authority, the desire for acceptance can become more intense, resulting in complex dynamics in hierarchical relationships.

Emotional Contagion and Connection

Emotional contagion, the phenomenon in which people replicate the feelings of those around them, is important in the social dynamics of approbation. Positive emotions like approbation and validation spread and lead to a sense of belonging. Individuals are naturally drawn to acts that elicit pleasant emotions in others, establishing a sense of belonging.

Understanding emotional contagion highlights the emotional roots of approval dynamics. In the search of approbation, the desire to convey happy emotions and maintain a harmonious social environment becomes a driving force.

Virtual Approval and Social Media

Social media platforms have become crucial to the social dynamics of approbation in the digital age. The virtual world magnifies the visibility of people's activities and accomplishments, creating a curated space for seeking acceptance. Likes, comments, and shares are tangible markers of acceptance that influence behavior both online and offline.

Understanding the impact of social media broadens the approval dynamics environment. Individuals navigating the intricacies of online validation add new aspects to social relationships as they seek virtual acceptance.

Punishment and Social Reinforcement

A system of reinforcement and punishment is involved in the social dynamics of approbation. Positive feedback reinforces behaviors that conform to cultural norms and gain approval, but deviations may result in disapproval and social penalties. The anticipation of reinforcement and the dread of punishment both contribute to the molding of behavior.

Understanding social reinforcement and punishment provides insight into the mechanisms that influence approval dynamics. Individuals learn to traverse the social environment by modifying their conduct in response to the repercussions of seeking or failing to obtain approval.

Balancing Individual Authenticity and Social Harmony

Individuals struggle to balance their real selves with the need for societal peace in the middle of the delicate social dynamics of approbation. The conflict between expressing oneself and adhering to cultural norms is a fundamental subject in the quest for acceptance. Finding a happy medium entails negotiating the complexity of authenticity while also acknowledging the impact of societal dynamics on interpersonal connections.

Understanding the delicate balance between individual authenticity and communal peace provides a more nuanced view of the challenges that people encounter. It encourages introspection on the decisions made in quest of approval, as well as the possibility of building meaningful connections while being loyal to one's individuality.

This comprehensive review of Chapter two sheds light on the complex social dynamics of acceptance, analyzing the psychological, cultural, and interpersonal aspects that influence the need to please. The following chapters will delve deeper into the emotional and mental effects of approval-seeking actions, as well as techniques for navigating these complicated relationships.

CHAPTER THREE

Characteristics of a People-Pleaser

This chapter of the book continues the examination by looking into the complex features that constitute a people-pleaser. Recognizing these characteristics is critical for anyone who wants to understand their behaviors or help others on their path to authenticity. A people-pleaser's traits encompass a variety of attitudes and patterns that manifest in numerous facets of life.

Excessive Need for Approval

An overwhelming demand for approval lies at the heart of the people-pleasers personality. Individuals with people-pleasing inclinations frequently seek external validation to an excessive extent. Others' acceptance becomes a main measure of self-worth, prompting activities designed to elicit favorable feedback.

Understanding the obsessive demand for acceptance sheds light on a people-pleaser's core feature. It reveals a deep insecurity or fear of rejection that feeds the need to please.

Difficulty Saying No

The difficulty in saying no is a distinguishing feature of people-pleasers. Individuals with people-pleasing inclinations find it difficult to set limits and deny requests, whether out of fear of disappointing others or a desire to preserve a favorable image. Fear of future confrontation or censure often motivates people's hesitation to say no.

Understanding the challenge of saying no illuminates the internal fight that people-pleasers confront. It reveals the tendency to put the needs of others before one's well-being.

Conflict Avoidance

People-pleasers are very opposed to conflict. Individuals will go to considerable measures to avoid any scenario that may lead to dissension due to the discomfort involved with disagreement or confrontation. People-pleasers value harmony and nice interactions, therefore conflict avoidance becomes a crucial characteristic.

Understanding conflict avoidance reveals the underlying dread of bad emotions and disrupted relationships that drive people-pleasers to tread carefully in interactions.

Over commitment and Overworking

Over commitment and overwork are common characteristics of people-pleasers. Individuals with people-pleasing inclinations take on more obligations than they can bear to meet the expectations of others. As people-pleasers seek to satisfy perceived duties, over commitment frequently leads to stress and exhaustion.

Understanding the pattern of over commitment sheds light on the desire to be perceived as trustworthy and helpful. It reflects how difficult it is for people-pleasers to create appropriate boundaries for themselves.

Difficulty Expressing Authentic Opinions

People-pleasers may find it difficult to express their true feelings. The dread of being disagreed with or disapproved of limits their ability to express their actual views and feelings. People-pleasers, on the other hand, may acquiesce to the opinions of others to maintain a sense of belonging and avoid potential conflict.

The difficulty in expressing real thoughts highlights the internal tension between the desire for authenticity and the fear of unwanted reactions from others.

Putting Others' Needs before Their Own

The persistent prioritization of others' needs over their own is a distinguishing feature of people-pleasers. People-pleasers routinely compromise their well-being to secure the comfort and pleasure of those around them, whether in personal relationships or professional situations.

Understanding the pattern of putting others' needs first reveals people-pleasers self-sacrificing character. It displays a notion that one's worth is determined by one's capacity to meet the wants and expectations of others.

Fear of Rejection

A people-pleaser's qualities include a profound dread of rejection. The prospect of being hated or shunned looms large, prompting people-pleasers to go to tremendous efforts to gain approval. This fear of rejection becomes a motivating factor in their actions and decisions.

Understanding people-pleasers fear of rejection provides important insight into their inner environment. It indicates the fragility and anxiety linked with the possibility of others' criticism.

Difficulty Setting Boundaries

People-pleasers frequently struggle to establish and maintain limits. The fear of upsetting others or being viewed as selfish inhibits their capacity to set time, energy, and resource boundaries. Setting limits is challenging, which contributes to the cycle of over commitment and overload.

Understanding the difficulty of setting limits sheds light on the hazy lines that exist between the demands of people-pleasers and the expectations of others. It shows the continual conflict between the desire for independence and the need to please.

Chronic Self-Doubt

People-pleasers frequently suffer from chronic self-doubt. Individuals with people-pleasing inclinations may have chronic worries about their worthiness and talents, despite external affirmation. Relying on outside approval as a measure of self-esteem continues a cycle of seeking reassurance.

Understanding chronic self-doubt highlights the underlying problems that people-pleasers experience. It emphasizes the need to develop internal self-worth independent of external validation.

Difficulty Receiving Criticism

Receiving criticism can be especially difficult for people-pleasers. Their sensitivity to criticism is increased by their fear of disappointing others or being seen adversely. People-pleasers may take criticism as a personal failure rather than accepting constructive input as a chance for improvement.

Understanding the difficulty of receiving criticism illustrates the fragile nature of people-pleasers self-esteem. It emphasizes the significance of cultivating resilience and a healthy response to feedback.

This thorough examination of this Chapter sheds light on the subtle traits that identify a people-pleaser. Recognizing these characteristics is an important step toward comprehending the motivations and behaviors linked with people-pleasing inclinations. The following chapters will dive into the emotional and mental repercussions of these characteristics, as well as solutions for breaking free from people-pleasing routines.

Identifying the Telltale Signs

Chapter three takes the reader on a voyage of self-awareness, providing a comprehensive guide to recognizing the unmistakable indications of people-pleasing. Recognizing these subtle indicators is an important step toward breaking free from routines of approval-seeking behavior. Individuals can acquire insight into their tendencies or offer support to those navigating the difficult environment of people-pleasing by identifying the indicators.

Subtle Language Patterns

Subtle linguistic patterns are one of the telltale symptoms of people-pleasing. People-pleasing individuals may regularly use language that seeks affirmation or avoids potential disputes. Phrases like "I guess," "I'm not sure, but," or "If you want" show a hesitation to express one's thoughts or preferences.

Identifying subtle linguistic patterns allows you to gain insight into the underlying drive to please others and preserve a positive image. Paying attention to these linguistic indicators might help you identify people-pleasing traits.

Reluctance to Express Disagreement

A hesitation to express dissent is an obvious symptom of people-pleasing. People-pleasers frequently agree with the beliefs and decisions of others, even when they disagree. This hesitation to express opposition is motivated by a fear of generating conflict or disappointment.

Recognizing a person's reluctance to express dissent reveals a critical indicator of people-pleasing conduct. It asks people to explore if their reluctance to disagree stems from a real shared viewpoint or from a desire to please.

Over apologizing

People-pleasers over apologize to appease others and escape potential judgment. Excessive apologizing, especially for trivial faults or events beyond one's control, is a telltale symptom of a predisposition to put the sentiments of others over one's own.

Identifying the pattern of over-apologizing reveals a deep need for praise as well as a fear of being viewed as a bother or nuisance. Individuals who are aware of this conduct can investigate the reasoning behind their apologies.

Discomfort with Receiving Compliments

Uneasiness with receiving compliments is a subtle indicator of people-pleasing. People-pleasing personalities may downplay or deflect compliments, attributing their accomplishments to external forces or others. The worry of being viewed as haughty or bringing attention to oneself causes this uneasiness.

Recognizing discomfort with praise indicates underlying self-esteem issues and a proclivity to seek external approval. It encourages people to consider their emotions in positive comments and their relationship with praise.

Ongoing Over commitments

People-pleasing is characterized by over commitment. People-pleasing personality types usually take on more tasks and responsibilities than they can fairly handle. This overextension is motivated by a desire to satisfy the expectations of others and avoid disappointing or disappointing those who want their assistance.

Individuals are prompted to review their capacity for tasks and obligations when they identify consistent over commitment. It indicates a need to set healthier boundaries and emphasize self-care over the need to impress.

Unwillingness to Disappoint Others

An unwillingness to disappoint others is a common indicator of people-pleasing. Individuals with people-pleasing inclinations will go to considerable lengths to meet the needs and desires of those around them, even if it means sacrificing their well-being. This reluctance to disappoint stems from a fear of unwanted reactions or rejection.

Recognizing the desire not to disappoint others sheds light on the emotional cost of pleasing others. It encourages people to question their intentions and evaluate the long-term consequences on their mental and emotional well-being.

Anxiety Surrounding Social Interactions

Anxiety about social encounters is common in people-pleasers. The fear of saying or doing the incorrect thing, along with the desire to be liked, causes increased uneasiness in social situations. This worry may take the form of a persistent desire for reassurance or a hesitation to share genuine opinions.

Identifying anxiety in social encounters allows people to investigate the underlying causes of their discomfort. It is an important milestone on the path to identifying and overcoming people-pleasing habits.

Chronic Self-Doubt

Chronic self-doubt is a common indicator of people-pleasing. Individuals constantly doubt their abilities, decisions, and worthiness, relying on external affirmation to alleviate their internal doubts. This persistent self-doubt becomes a driving force in the quest for approval.

Recognizing chronic self-doubt forces people to tackle the underlying insecurities that drive people-pleasing behavior.

It promotes growing inner self-worth independent of external validation.

Sacrificing Personal Values

People-pleasers frequently forsake their ideals to meet the expectations of others. This compromise may include decisions, beliefs, or actions that contradict one's true self. The willingness to give up personal ideals is an indication of an internal conflict between authenticity and the desire for external approval.

Identifying the sacrifice of personal ideals provides an important opportunity for self-reflection. It encourages people to consider the alignment between their behaviors and their basic beliefs, resulting in a better understanding of the consequences of people-pleasing.

Lack of Assertiveness

A lack of assertiveness is a distinguishing feature of people-pleasing. People-pleasing personalities may struggle to assert their demands, preferences, or boundaries. The unwillingness to assert oneself originates from a fear of offending people or inciting conflict.

Recognizing a lack of assertiveness causes people to assess their capacity to advocate for themselves. It emphasizes the need to establish assertiveness as a critical ability in breaking out from people-pleasing patterns.

This in-depth examination this section offers useful insights on spotting the unmistakable characteristics of people-pleasing. Understanding these tiny clues is an important step on the path to self-discovery and honesty. The following chapters will explore deeper into the emotional and mental ramifications of these indications, as well as solutions for breaking free from people-pleasing routines.

Unraveling the Layers of Motivation

Chapter three looks deeper into the many levels of motivation that underpin people-pleasing activities. Understanding these motivations is critical for people who want to break free from approval-seeking routines and go on a path of honesty. Exploring the psychological, emotional, and cultural aspects that motivate the need for acceptance is part of unraveling the layers of motivation.

Intrinsic Motivations for Connection

Intrinsic impulses for connection are at the heart of people-pleasing. Humans have an inbuilt desire for social connection and a sense of belonging. People-pleasing behaviors may be exhibited by people-pleasers as a sincere expression of their desire to connect with others and establish healthy relationships. Distinguishing between healthy, intrinsic desires for connection and the compulsive need for acceptance is required to unravel this layer.

Investigating innate reasons for connection encourages people to evaluate the legitimacy of their social connections. It promotes the formation of true bonds based on mutual understanding and shared ideals.

Fear of Abandonment and Isolation

The fear of desertion and loneliness is a major motivator in people-pleasing. Individuals with people-pleasing inclinations may have deep-seated anxieties of rejection or exclusion. The quest for approval serves as a protective mechanism against the perceived threat of abandonment, promoting activities aimed at sustaining social bonds.

Addressing the underlying worries that underlie approval-seeking is necessary for unraveling the layer of abandonment dread. It encourages people to look into healthier ways of coping with solitude and building a sense of internal stability.

External Validation as a Source of Self-Worth

For people-pleasers, external affirmation adds a substantial dimension of drive. Seeking approval becomes a technique for gaining self-esteem and recognition from others. Recognizing the reliance on external input as a measure of personal value and investigating avenues for fostering internal self-esteem are required to unravel this layer.

Investigating the importance of external validation causes people to shift their attention from external opinions to internal sources of self-worth. It promotes the development of a more resilient and genuine feeling of worth.

Coping Mechanism for Anxiety and Uncertainty

People-pleasing is frequently used as a coping strategy for worry and uncertainty. Individuals may experience increased anxiety as a result of their fear of social judgment or disapproval, leading them to engage in approval-seeking actions as a means to cope with their uncomfortable feelings. Unravel this layer by developing healthier coping mechanisms to address underlying worries.

Investigating people-pleasing as a coping technique leads to the development of adaptive strategies for dealing with stress and uncertainty. It promotes the development of resilience and emotional well-being in the absence of external validation.

Cultural Conditioning and Societal Norms

People-pleasers are motivated by a layer of cultural upbringing and societal conventions. Individuals are taught from a young age to conform to cultural ideals of civility, agreeability, and social peace. Recognizing the impact of cultural influences on approval-seeking behaviors and reassessing the alignment between personal ideals and societal standards are required to unravel this layer.

Exploring cultural conditioning forces people to strike a balance between adhering to societal conventions and expressing their true selves. Shaping approval dynamics, encourages a deeper awareness of the societal context.

Desire for Harmonious Relationships

A real desire for peaceful relationships adds drive to people-pleasing. People-pleasers may engage in approval-seeking behaviors to establish happy and conflict-free connections. Untangling this layer entails differentiating between healthy relationship-building and the temptation to prefer harmony over real self-expression.

Investigating the desire for harmonious relationships leads to the development of effective communication skills and conflict-resolution solutions. It promotes the formation of relationships based on open communication and mutual understanding.

Learned Behaviors from Childhood

Childhood learned actions provide a huge layer of incentive for people-pleasers. The development of approval-seeking tendencies is influenced by early experiences, parenting, and parental expectations. Unraveling this layer entails reflecting on how childhood events have influenced current behavior and making conscious efforts to break free from learned behaviors.

Investigating taught habits from childhood leads to an examination of the roots of approval-seeking inclinations. It promotes the process of unlearning established behaviors and the development of fresh, real approaches to relationships.

Perceived Lack of Alternative Strategies

A perceived lack of alternate tactics for navigating social situations may inspire people-pleasers. These activities may be motivated by the assumption that gaining acceptance is the only effective method to achieve favorable outcomes. Unraveling this layer entails broadening one's repertoire of interpersonal abilities and establishing a wide range of communication tactics.

Exploring the perceived lack of alternate communication tactics drives individuals to investigate and use more forceful, honest communication approaches. It promotes a proactive approach to learning a variety of abilities for navigating social dynamics.

Fear of Rejection and Social Exclusion

Fear of rejection and social marginalization is a powerful motivator for people-pleasing. People will go to tremendous lengths to avoid circumstances that may result in rejection or exclusion from social groupings. Untangling this layer entails confronting and dealing with the underlying fear of undesirable social outcomes.

Exploring the fear of rejection leads to the development of resilience and coping methods for dealing with prospective social setbacks. It promotes a transition from avoidance to more bold and real participation in social encounters.

Authority Figures' Recognition and Affirmation

People-pleasers are motivated by recognition and affirmation from authority figures. It is possible to seek approval from individuals in positions of authority to confirm one's competence and worth. Unraveling this layer entails reassessing the importance of external recognition and validating one's talents independently of authority figures.

Investigating the desire for acknowledgment prompts people to recognize their intrinsic worth and accomplishments. It promotes the development of self-affirmation activities that lead to a stronger sense of self.

This in-depth look dives into the complex levels of motivation that drive people-pleasing activities. Unraveling these layers is an important step toward honesty and breaking free from approval-seeking routines. The following chapters will go deeper into the emotional and mental ramifications of these motives, as well as ways for cultivating true connections and self-discovery.

CHAPTER FOUR

The Cost of People-Pleasing

As we progress through Chapter four, our attention switches to a critical analysis of the significant consequences associated with the prevalent habit of people-pleasing. While getting approval and sustaining harmonious relationships may appear tempting, the toll it takes on many aspects of one's life should not be ignored. The goal of this chapter is to thoroughly uncover the multiple costs associated with people-pleasing practices. Each cost holds weight and significance in the journey toward self-discovery and authenticity, from emotional and mental strain to the erosion of authenticity and self-identity. By thoroughly investigating these expenses, we equip ourselves to make informed decisions and go on a road that values genuine connection, mental well-being, and the fulfillment of our authentic selves. Let us navigate the perilous terrain of the expenses of pleasing others, taking into account the ramifications for our emotional, mental, and relationship health.

The Emotional Cost of Inner Turmoil

People-pleasing, while presenting an appearance of harmony and cooperation at first, exacts a significant emotional toll on individuals. This chapter digs into the complex topography of the emotional cost of people-pleasing, revealing the inner agony that often lurks under the surface.

The Suppression Dilemma

The repression of genuine feelings is at the heart of the emotional toll. People-pleasers, motivated by the need to maintain exterior harmony, frequently repress actual feelings to avoid conflict or condemnation. This repression produces an internal conflict as people struggle to reconcile the tension between presenting a composed façade and the chaos seething within.

Frustration and Resentment

The emotional toll manifests as a quiet undertone of resentment and irritation. The inability to communicate actual emotions causes a buildup of bad sensations. This reservoir of suppressed emotions can reach a tipping point over time, resulting in an emotional storm that gets increasingly difficult to navigate.

Loss of Self-Expression

Constantly putting others' sentiments ahead of one's leads to a gradual lack of self-expression. The emotional cost includes a reduced ability to communicate authentically with oneself. People-pleasers may become divorced from their inner feelings, leaving them with a sense of emptiness and a longing for genuine self-expression.

Internal Conflict and Guilt

Internal turmoil becomes a constant companion for people-pleasers as they navigate the difficult balance of meeting others' expectations. The conflict comes from a schism between the true self and the self-shaped by external approval demands. This internal strife is sometimes accompanied by pervasive feelings of guilt, which result from a perceived inability to meet the expectations of others.

Anxiety and Overwhelm

The emotional toll includes increased worry and a general sensation of overload. Constantly managing social encounters to please others fosters a feeling of constant attention and apprehension. The dread of disappointing or being rejected grows stronger, adding to an elevated emotional state.

Emotional Exhaustion

Emotional weariness is the result of emotional suppression, internal conflict, and anxiety. People-pleasers may become cognitively and emotionally exhausted as they negotiate the intricate web of pleasing others. This emotional weariness might impair one's ability to deal with life's obstacles and appreciate genuine joy.

Navigating Inner Turmoil

In the emotional toll of people-pleasing, navigating inner anguish becomes a prominent focus. Individuals become involved in a complex web of emotions, swinging between the need for external approval and the desire for genuine self-expression. Recognizing and handling this inner struggle is a critical first step toward breaking free from the emotional costs of pleasing others.

This examination of the emotional cost offers the groundwork for comprehending the complex layers of inner turmoil connected with people-pleasing activities. The next parts will go deeper into ways for navigating and transcending this emotional environment, allowing people to restore their authenticity and emotional well-being.

Mental Strain: The Hidden Consequences

In the intricate exploration of the costs of people-pleasing, Chapter four unveils the hidden consequences embedded in the realm of mental strain. Underneath the surface of pleasing others is a complicated interaction of ideas and emotions, which frequently results in a subtle but substantial toll on mental health. This chapter digs into the nuances of mental strain, revealing its hidden effects and putting light on its complex impact on individuals.

The Perpetual Balancing Act

The constant balancing act that humans perform is at the heart of mental strain in the context of people-pleasing. Struggling to meet external expectations while dealing with one's genuine self creates a mental tightrope that necessitates ongoing cognitive and emotional exertion. The strain arises as individuals straddle the fine line between adhering to the desires of others and expressing their genuine selves.

Cognitive Dissonance

Cognitive dissonance results from the tension between the urge to impress and the internal turmoil caused by compromised authenticity. People-pleasers may become entangled in a web of competing thoughts and beliefs, unable to reconcile the gap between their behaviors and actual objectives. This cognitive contradiction contributes greatly to the mental strain felt.

Anxiety and Anticipation

Anticipating the responses and expectations of others causes people-pleasers to get anxious. The constant fear of being rejected or disappointed causes a persistent sense of anxiety. Anxiety becomes a quiet companion, interfering with cognitive functions and adding to a general sensation of unease.

Over commitment and Exhaustion

The desire to please frequently leads to over-commitment, as people stretch themselves thin in an attempt to meet several obligations. The emotional and physical tiredness that results intensifies the strain. Over-commitment fosters burnout, affecting not only people's ability to please but also their overall cognitive performance and resilience.

Self-Reflection and Self-Doubt

Self-reflection and self-doubt are inextricably tied to mental distress. People-pleasers constantly monitor themselves to gain external validation. This increased self-awareness can lead to self-doubt as people question their authenticity and worthiness, which contributes to a fragile mental state.

Emotional Turmoil

Emotional turbulence is frequently caused by an undertone of mental tension. Suppressing true emotions while balancing pleasing others creates a chaotic emotional terrain. As individuals cope with the complexities of their internal environment, the strain manifests as episodes of frustration, melancholy, or emotional overwhelm.

Impact on Decision-Making

The influence of mental strain extends to decision-making. People-pleasers who are entangled in a web of external expectations may find it difficult to make decisions that are in line with their actual goals. The mental weight of contemplating others' preferences can distort judgment and impair the ability to make choices that are true to oneself.

The Toll on Cognitive Resources

The drain on cognitive resources is an unnoticed side effect of mental pressure. Juggling others' expectations and negotiating the nuances of people-pleasing consumes mental resources. This depletion can impair cognitive performance, affecting tasks requiring focus, creativity, and problem-solving.

Breaking the Cycle

Breaking away from the hidden consequences of mental tension becomes a critical component of the path to authenticity. This chapter serves as a primer for comprehending the complexities of mental strain and offers suggestions for breaking the loop. Individuals can regain mental well-being and pave the way for a more authentic and fulfilled existence by uncovering the hidden repercussions.

As we navigate the depths of mental strain in the context of people-pleasing, the following sections will go deeper into tactics for reducing its influence and cultivating a robust and authentic mental environment.

CHAPTER FIVE

Striking a Balance: The Importance of Boundaries

Chapter five of the journey toward authenticity and self-discovery focuses on a critical aspect—achieving balance through the setting of healthy limits. People-pleasing frequently blurs the borders between self and others, making it critical to investigate the relevance of setting and maintaining boundaries. This chapter explores the complex landscape of boundaries, delving into their function in creating authentic connections, sustaining mental health, and empowering individuals to recover responsibility for their lives.

Defining Boundaries

It is critical to establish boundaries before embarking on this journey. Boundaries are the invisible but powerful lines that separate oneself from others. They act as a compass, leading people through interpersonal dynamics, controlling expectations, and protecting their emotional and mental well-being.

The Spectrum of Boundaries

Understanding that there are boundaries on a spectrum is critical. Individuals traverse a wide spectrum of limits in their interactions, from physical boundaries that define personal space to emotional boundaries that protect one's innermost sentiments. Recognizing the mobility of these limits and customizing them to suit personal ideals and comfort levels is the key to striking a balance.

The Connection between Boundaries and Authenticity

The significant connection between boundaries and authenticity is at the center of this chapter. Setting and maintaining boundaries is a key act of self-affirmation, allowing individuals to express their genuine selves without yielding to external influences. Boundaries serve as the framework around which authenticity is constructed.

Navigating External Expectations

People-pleasers frequently struggle under the weight of external expectations. To navigate these expectations, it is necessary to establish clear limits. It enables people to distinguish between accommodating others without jeopardizing their well-being and falling into the trap of overcommitting to please.

Fostering Genuine Connections

Boundaries serve as protectors of true connections. Individuals invite people to engage with them truly by outlining the space for true self-expression. Relationships with healthy boundaries are built on mutual respect, understanding, and a shared commitment to authenticity.

Preserving Mental Well-Being

Boundaries have a significant impact on mental well-being. Individuals who learn to articulate and maintain boundaries build a defense against emotional depletion, burnout, and the stress of always pleasing others. Through boundary setting, preserving mental well-being becomes a conscious act of self-care.

Empowering Individuals

Finally, establishing boundaries and striking a balance is an empowering process. It is a statement of self-worth, agency, and the realization that true living necessitates a deliberate and considered approach to interpersonal dynamics. This chapter serves as a guide, providing insights into the art of establishing boundaries and navigating the delicate dance between self and others.

Let us examine the transformational power of boundaries as we go into Chapter five, revealing a road toward honesty, true connections, and the happy coexistence of individuality within the complicated web of relationships.

The Role of Healthy Boundaries

The focus of Chapter five developing story switches to a transformative element—the construction and maintenance of healthy boundaries. Understanding the critical role of boundaries becomes critical when we investigate the complexities of people-pleasing. This chapter looks deeply into the multidimensional relevance of healthy boundaries, revealing their function in establishing authentic connections, protecting mental health, and helping individuals navigate the delicate dance between self and others.

Defining Healthy Boundaries

The determination of appropriate boundaries is at the heart of our investigation. Healthy borders, as opposed to solid barriers that isolate, are dynamic and permeable structures that promote happy cohabitation between self and others. They act as a compass, guiding people through interpersonal relationships with clarity, respect, and a firm commitment to honesty.

Nurturing Self-Respect

Healthy boundaries protect one's self-esteem. Individuals construct an atmosphere that values their intrinsic worth by clearly establishing the boundaries of acceptable behavior. As individuals negotiate relationships from a place of intrinsic value, self-respect becomes the cornerstone of authentic living.

Empowering Personal Agency

Setting healthy limits is a powerful expression of human agency. It shifts the locus of power from external forces to the individual, allowing them to select how they interact with the world consciously. This empowerment prepares the path for deliberate life, in which individuals confidently declare their desires, needs, and values.

Fostering Genuine Connections

The ability of healthy limits to build genuine interactions is central to their purpose. Individuals invite people to engage with them truly by outlining the space for true self-expression. Healthy boundaries foster a relational environment in which mutual respect, understanding, and acceptance thrive, laying the framework for meaningful and true partnerships.

Balancing Autonomy and Connection

The significance of healthy limits in balancing autonomy and connection is one of their subtle elements. Individuality is preserved by autonomy, yet healthy connections thrive when boundaries are stated and respected. The delicate balance strikes a chord between respecting personal space and engaging in mutually fulfilling interactions.

Protecting Mental and Emotional Well-Being

Healthy boundaries provide a significant protective function in mental and emotional well-being. Individuals develop a shield against burnout, emotional tiredness, and the hidden costs of people-pleasing by putting explicit limits on the emotional energy invested in pleasing others. Healthy boundaries become an essential component of self-care, protecting the value of mental and emotional resources.

Enhancing Communication

Communication is critical in maintaining healthy limits. Effectively communicating one's limits and expectations develops an open and mutually respectful atmosphere. Healthy boundaries improve communication by providing a framework for expressing needs, addressing issues, and engaging in discussion that respects all participants' authenticity.

Building Self-Trust

Individuals embark on a transformative path toward self-trust as they learn to articulate and enforce healthy limits. This self-trust develops into a reservoir of resilience, anchoring people in their authenticity and leading them through the intricacies of interpersonal dynamics. Healthy limits foster a strong sense of self-assurance and reliance.

Embracing Change and Growth

Healthy limits go beyond simply maintaining the status quo; they embrace change and progress. Individuals' boundaries shift as they get older. Healthy boundaries adapt to changing circumstances, helping people negotiate the ever-changing landscape of personal growth with flexibility and sincerity.

The Art of Boundary Setting

Setting healthy limits is an art that takes time and self-awareness to master. This chapter acts as a primer, providing insights into the complexities of boundary setting. Boundary setting becomes a transforming ability on the road toward authenticity and balanced relationships, from clearly stating expectations to gracefully demanding one's demands.

As we continue to look into healthy boundaries, the next sections will provide further ways for growing and sustaining these crucial structures. The function of healthy boundaries emerges as a vital aspect in the search for a more authentic and satisfying existence, from the delicate dance of balancing autonomy with connection to the transformational force of self-trust.

Saying "No" Without Feeling Guilty

In the final half of Chapter Five, we look at the transforming ability of saying "No" without feeling guilty. This delicate art is an important part of creating and sustaining empowered limits, as well as living an authentic life.

The Liberating Power of Boundaries

Saying "No" without feeling guilty necessitates a thorough awareness of the freeing power of boundaries. Boundaries are not obstacles; they are the framework for self-respect and self-care. This section emphasizes the importance of setting healthy boundaries as an act of empowerment that allows people to navigate life with clarity and purpose.

Boundaries offer the framework for true living to flourish. They define the area in which personal beliefs and priorities take precedence, hence protecting one's authenticity. When people accept that saying "No" is an expression of their limits, guilt evolves into a sense of self-worth.

Guilt's Psychology

Before you can master the skill of saying "No" without feeling guilty, you must first understand the psychology of guilt. Guilt is frequently caused by societal expectations, a desire for external praise, or an innate urge to please others. This section delves into the origins of guilt, offering light on its origins and impact on decision-making.

Understanding the psychology of guilt is essential for overcoming it. It entails confronting erroneous ideas and societal standards that perpetuate shame linked with establishing limits. Individuals can improve their relationship by saying "No" by breaking these engrained tendencies.

Saying "No" Strategies Empowered

Adopting particular techniques that empower rather than reduce is required to master the art of saying "No" without guilt. This section provides practical advice on successful communication, assertiveness, and structuring responses with empathy.

Communication Clarity: Clearly stating the grounds for the refusal is a strong strategy. When others understand why you said "No," it creates a sense of transparency and respect.

Assertiveness methods: Learning assertiveness methods will help you articulate your requirements while still respecting the needs of others. Maintaining eye contact, utilizing confident body language, and speaking in a calm yet forceful tone are all examples of this.

Embracing Empathy: Saying "No" with empathy is appreciating the other person's point of view while remaining steadfast in one's decision. It promotes comprehension and reduces the likelihood of misconceptions.

The Transformational Impact

Individuals who learn to say "No" without feeling guilty have a huge impact on their lives. This section delves into the knock-on consequences, such as better relationships, increased self-esteem, and a more true connection with personal beliefs.

The ability to say "No" without feeling guilty is not only a self-preservation act, but it is also a gift to others. It lays the groundwork for open communication, allowing for deeper ties based on mutual respect. Beyond individual well-being, the transformation has a positive rippling effect on the social dynamics of relationships.

It is well known that saying "No" without guilt is a talent that transcends the particular act—it is an embodiment of empowered limits and a commitment to true life. Individuals who manage the delicate dance of setting boundaries with clarity and empathy prepare the way for a life in which saying "No" authentically becomes a booming statement of self-worth and integrity. This mastery is more than a skill; it is a liberation—a declaration that authenticity is respected and protected with unflinching strength and elegance.

CHAPTER SIX

Doing What's Right vs. Pleasing Everyone

As we venture into Chapter six, the focal point shifts towards the essential dichotomy of doing what's right versus the perpetual pursuit of pleasing everyone. This chapter delves into the intricacies of aligning actions with personal values, exploring the problems created by the desire to please others and the critical importance of being loyal to one's underlying views. The transforming potential of recognizing the difference between external acceptance and real alignment of actions with deeply held beliefs is at the heart of this research.

The Dilemma of External Approval

The conflict between doing what is right and pleasing everyone is frequently rooted in the quest for external approval. The human inclination to seek approval and acceptance from others can lead to a perpetual conflict between upholding personal ideals and adhering to cultural norms. Recognizing and resolving this quandary is critical to cultivating a sense of authenticity and purpose.

The Allure of Pleasing Everyone

The temptation of pleasing everyone is a powerful magnet that draws people into the complicated web of people-pleasing. The desire for external validation, harmonious relationships, and cultural acceptance can overwhelm the necessity of being true to one's ideals. The alluring nature of people-pleasing inclinations and their impact on true life are discussed in this section of the chapter.

Defining Personal Values

The fundamental understanding of personal values is at the heart of connecting behaviors with essential beliefs. Personal values are defined in this section as profoundly held concepts and convictions that govern decision-making and shape individual identity. Clarifying own beliefs is an important step in handling the tension between doing what is right and pleasing others.

The Impact of External Validation

A prominent subject is the effect of external evaluation on the alignment of behaviors with personal ideals. The chapter investigates how relying on external acceptance can lead to a deviation from authentic life, as people emphasize pleasing others over sticking to their firmly held convictions. Understanding the impact of one's acts is critical for reclaiming agency over one's actions.

The Liberation of Authentic Alignment

Authentic alignment with personal values emerges as a liberating force on the path to doing the right thing. This part explores the liberation that comes from making decisions based on inner convictions rather than external expectations. It investigates the empowerment that occurs when an individual's activities mirror their real values, producing a sense of purpose and fulfillment.

The Challenges of Disapproval

Aligning behaviors with personal ideals frequently brings criticism from others. This section of the chapter investigates the anxiety and discomfort caused by impending criticism or rejection. It delves into ways to overcome these obstacles while remaining devoted to authentic living and the pursuit of what is right.

Embracing Uniqueness

The conflict between doing what is right and pleasing everyone is also linked to embracing one's individuality. This section encourages people to embrace their uniqueness and recognizes that being authentic frequently entails making decisions that may not be popular with everyone. Accepting one's individuality becomes a cornerstone in the pursuit of personal values.

Defying Societal Norms

The evaluation of societal norms is part of the exploration of doing what is right versus pleasing everyone. This section of the text dives into the bravery required to resist societal norms when they contradict personal ideals. It honors the fortitude of those who choose authenticity over conformity.

Strategies for Authentic Alignment

The chapter finishes with practical ideas for connecting behaviors with basic beliefs in an honest way. It provides advice on developing self-awareness, establishing personal beliefs, and making deliberate decisions that reflect authenticity. These solutions enable individuals to manage the dichotomy's intricacies, producing a more purposeful and values-driven life.

Let us explore the intricate interplay between doing what is right and the attraction of pleasing everyone as we begin Chapter six, seeking a path that matches actions with the basic ideas that determine individuality and authenticity.

Defining Personal Values

The foundation of the inquiry of doing what is right versus the widespread desire to please everyone is a full grasp of personal values. This section of Chapter six looks into the complexities of defining personal values, which is an important step in managing the difficult interaction between authenticity and external expectations.

The Essence of Personal Values

Every person has a unique collection of principles, beliefs, and convictions that affect decision-making and determine identity. Individuals' values act as a compass, guiding them in identifying what is truly essential and significant to them. This essence is the foundation of real living and serves as an anchor amid the turbulent sea of external influences.

Identifying Core Principles

Personal values must be defined via introspection and self-discovery. Individuals engage in a quest to discover the underlying concepts that are profoundly connected to their actual selves. These principles could include things like honesty, integrity, compassion, freedom, justice, or any other deeply held ideals.

Cultivating Self-Awareness

Self-awareness is an essential component of defining personal ideals. This entails a thorough examination of one's ideas, motivations, and priorities. Self-awareness reveals the layers of indoctrination, cultural influences, and personal experiences that determine people's values. Individuals obtain clarity on what is genuinely important to them through reflection.

Prioritizing Value

While personal values vary and are unique, prioritizing them is an important step. Individuals must determine which values are foundational to their identity and decision-making because not all values have equal weight. Prioritizing values establishes a hierarchy that assists people in making decisions that are consistent with their most strongly held convictions.

The Fluid Nature of Values

It is critical to remember that personal values do not remain constant; they change and adapt throughout time. Values are variable because of life events, personal growth, and changing circumstances. This section examines the dynamic nature of values and emphasizes the significance of reassessing and improving them regularly to maintain continuing harmony with authentic living.

Aligning Values with Actions

Personal value definition is more than just an academic exercise; it also entails the practical alignment of ideals with actions. Individuals must endeavor to live by their values, making choices and actions that are consistent with the ideals they cherish. The section delves into the transforming effect of value alignment in generating authenticity and purpose.

Overcoming External Influences

External influences, societal conventions, and the need for approval can make defining and sticking to personal beliefs difficult. This section of the chapter dives into ways to deal with external pressures, creating resilience in the face of societal expectations, and empowering individuals to remain loyal to their principles even in the face of potential criticism.

Embracing Diversity of Values

Individuals must recognize and appreciate the range of values in others as they determine their particular values. This section discusses the significance of accepting diverse viewpoints and cultivating an accepting society that allows individuals to authentically express their ideas without condemnation.

Living Authentically Through Values

Living truthfully is the ultimate goal of identifying personal beliefs. This entails incorporating values into all parts of life, including relationships, work, decision-making, and personal development. The section encourages people to live their principles daily, creating a life that reflects the genuine core of who they are.

As we navigate the landscape of personal values within Chapter six, the subsequent sections will further unravel the challenges and triumphs of aligning actions with core beliefs. Doing what is right is a purposeful and intentional effort guided by the compass of personal values.

Aligning Actions with Core Beliefs

As we progress through Chapter six, the last section takes shape, concentrating on the transforming path of aligning actions with basic beliefs. This part delves into the complexities of converting personal values into intentional choices and behaviors, managing the hurdles that arise, and enjoying the authenticity that emerges when actions smoothly fit with strongly held principles.

The Power of Intentional Choices

The power of intentional decisions lies at the heart of aligning behaviors with core beliefs. Individuals start on a conscious path in which they make decisions that align with their unique values. This entails becoming more conscious of the options available in daily life and committing to choosing pathways that honor the essence of one's values.

Authentic Living in Daily Choices

Authentic life is not limited to spectacular acts but pervades the fabric of daily decisions. This section looks at how aligning behaviors with basic values emerges in the tiny decisions people make, such as how they communicate and prioritize their time, as well as the ethical issues entrenched in their professional and personal lives.

Navigating Challenges and Divergence

The path of aligning actions with basic values is not without difficulties. External pressures, competing priorities, and unforeseen events may put the commitment to authentic living to the test. This section of the chapter dives into ways for overcoming problems and dealing with instances of divergence, focusing on resilience and the ability to realign with essential ideas.

The Ripple Effect in Relationships

The alignment of actions with basic ideas has a significant impact on relationships. This section investigates how individual choices contribute to the development of meaningful bonds. Authentic living catalyzes the development of relationships based on mutual respect, understanding, and acceptance of varied values.

Professional and Ethical Alignment

For many, the job is a critical arena in which values are realized. In a professional environment, aligning activities with core beliefs entails merging personal values with ethical issues. This section of the chapter investigates the transformative impact of values-driven decision-making on professional development, fulfillment, and ethical behavior.

Staying True to Core Beliefs in Adversity

Adversity frequently puts one's devotion to key ideas to the test. This section looks at how people can stay true to their ideals in the face of obstacles, failures, and external influences. The ability to endure difficulties while maintaining essential values demonstrates the depth of one's dedication to true living.

The Continuous Journey of Alignment

The road of aligning actions with core values is a never-ending process of growth and self-discovery. This section of the chapter encourages people to think of alignment as an ongoing journey, recognizing that values change and that conscious choices contribute to a dynamic and authentic existence.

Embracing Authenticity

Finally, aligning activities with basic values leads to the acceptance of authenticity. This part recognizes the transforming potential of living truthfully, as well as the liberation that comes from choosing decisions that are in line with one's actual nature. In navigating the challenges of doing what is right versus pleasing everyone, authenticity becomes a guiding principle.

Impact on Personal Well-Being

Aligning activities with basic values has a significant impact on personal happiness. This section of the chapter delves into how authenticity promotes a sense of purpose, fulfillment, and inner peace. The alignment of behaviors and values becomes a source of resilience and mental health.

Inspiring Others through Authentic Living

The ripple effect of authentic living extends beyond individual well-being. This section investigates how behaviors that are consistent with core convictions might inspire others. Individuals who model authenticity help to build a culture that recognizes and embraces a variety of thoughts, inspiring others to go on their journey of aligning actions with core convictions

As Chapter six concludes, the insights shared serve as a guide for individuals navigating the intricate dance between doing what's right and the temptation to please everyone. The process of defining personal values and connecting behaviors with basic convictions transforms into a transforming quest that fosters authenticity, purpose, and a more meaningful way of life. The following chapters will deepen the varied investigation of true living and the complexity of the human experience.

CHAPTER SEVEN

Breaking Free: Breaking Free from People-Pleasing

As we enter Chapter seven, the focus switches to a transformative exploration—liberation from the all-encompassing grip of people-pleasing. This chapter offers a light of hope for anyone wishing to break free from the suffocating cycle of seeking external approval and compromising authenticity for the comfort of others. It begins with a critical recognition of the people-pleasing pattern and then delves into actionable self-empowerment tactics, leading the road to a genuine and free existence.

Acknowledging the Pattern

The path to liberty begins with a bold recognition of the people-pleasing pattern. This section establishes the framework for the following sections by allowing individuals to reflect on their behavioral inclinations, recognizing occasions where the drive to please others has taken precedence over personal well-being. Acknowledgement becomes the foundation for breaking bad behaviors and launching radical change.

Self-Reflection

Self-reflection is an effective method for recognizing the people-pleasing pattern. It entails a thorough assessment of previous acts, reasons, and decisions. Individuals get an understanding on the nuanced ways in which they have prioritized external affirmation through introspection. This self-awareness serves as a trigger for breaking free from the pattern and reclaiming agency.

Recognizing Behavioral Triggers

It is critical to understand the triggers that activate people-pleasing behaviors. This section of the chapter assists readers in identifying certain situations, emotions, or relationships that prompt a default response of seeking approval. Identifying these triggers allows individuals to gain insight into the pattern's roots and prepares them with the knowledge required for effective emancipation.

Embracing Vulnerability

Recognizing the people-pleasing habit necessitates embracing vulnerability. This section delves into the discomfort connected with recognizing patterns of conduct that may not be consistent with one's real self. Accepting vulnerability is a significant step in overcoming the fear of judgment and external disapproval.

Understanding the Roots

Understanding the roots of people-pleasing is vital for breaking away from it. This section digs into the psychological, social, and cultural factors that influence the development of people-pleasing inclinations.

Societal Expectations

Investigate how societal expectations, cultural norms, and familial influences influence the desire to please others. Understanding the external forces that contribute to the pattern gives light to the intricate interplay between individual decisions and societal obligations.

Fear of Rejection

Examine the fundamental fear of rejection that frequently underpins people-pleasing. Unpack the emotional layers associated with the need for acceptance and approval, and recognize how fear may be a powerful driver in perpetuating the pattern.

Learned Behavior

Recognize that people-pleasing is a taught behavior, especially if it was modeled in early relationships. This section invites people to consider their upbringing and interpersonal interactions, which may have led to the development of people-pleasing inclinations.

Breaking Down Fear and Guilt

Fear and guilt operate as unseen chains, keeping people in the people-pleasing loop. This section of the chapter deconstructs these feelings, providing insights for overcoming false fears of rejection and the guilt associated with setting limits.

Challenging Fear

Individuals are led through ways for confronting and conquering their fear of rejection. This entails reframing negative ideas, strengthening resilience, and establishing a mindset that values authentic living over external affirmation.

Rethinking Guilt

Investigate the sources of guilt connected with establishing boundaries or prioritizing personal needs. Strategies for reconsidering guilt are discussed, with an emphasis on self-compassion and the realization that setting boundaries is an act of self-respect, not selfishness.

Strategies for Self-Empowerment

This portion of the chapter exposes a comprehensive collection of tactics for self-empowerment—key aspects in the road toward liberation from people-pleasing—as pillars.

Setting Clear Boundaries

Setting clear limits becomes a self-advocacy effort that is empowering. This method assists individuals in assertively defining and conveying limits, creating autonomy and signaling a commitment to authentic living.

Practicing Saying "No"

The ability to firmly say "no" is a critical component of self-empowerment. Practical approaches are investigated, helping individuals to handle the unpleasantness of refuse while emphasizing their genuine needs.

Cultivating Self-Compassion

Self-compassion is a loving factor that promotes self-esteem. This section of the text looks into self-compassion tactics, highlighting their significance in resilience, overcoming setbacks, and maintaining momentum in the emancipation process.

Embracing Imperfection

Accepting imperfections is part of the freedom path. This method helps people to let go of their excessive expectations of perfection, creating an environment where authenticity thrives and fear of judgment fades.

Building a Supportive Network

Self-empowerment requires the creation of a supporting environment. This section discusses the significance of surrounding oneself with others who respect boundaries, promote authenticity, and contribute to the liberation process.

Celebrating Small Wins

Small victories are recognized and celebrated as a motivational strategy. Individuals are encouraged to recognize their progress, so reinforcing the positive actions they have taken toward breaking free from people-pleasing.

The ideas provided serve as a road map for those seeking to break free from the suffocating habits of people-pleasing. Recognizing the pattern, understanding its causes, and practicing self-empowerment tactics form the foundation for a genuine and liberated existence. The following sections will continue to delve into the complexities of the human experience and the numerous dimensions of real living.

Acknowledging the Pattern

As we embark on chapter seven, the trajectory of our exploration takes a transformative turn, focusing on the liberation from the pervasive grip of people-pleasing. This essential chapter begins with an important step: recognizing the deep and often subtle habit of seeking external approval at the expense of authenticity. We go into the complexities of fully accepting the people-pleasing pattern, comprehending its expressions, and embarking on a transforming journey toward self-awareness and empowerment in these pages.

The Importance of Acknowledgment

Recognizing the people-pleasing habit is a crucial step in the freedom journey. This section emphasizes the transforming effect of conscious recognition of ingrained practices. Acknowledgement is not only daring, but it also opens the door to self-discovery and the quest for a more true existence.

Recognizing Behavioral Cues

The path to liberty begins with the subtle art of identifying behavioral clues that indicate people-pleasing inclinations. Individuals are urged to reflect on previous interactions, decisions, and instances where the desire for external approval influenced choices. Recognizing these cues is the first step toward comprehending the pattern's complexities.

Reflective self-inquiry is a potent tool for self-awareness. Introspective exercises are used to urge individuals to investigate the motivations behind their acts, the feelings associated with people-pleasing, and the influence of these behaviors on their overall well-being. Reflective self-inquiry prepares the way for a more in-depth knowledge of the pattern.

Embracing Vulnerability

Acceptance necessitates a willingness to embrace vulnerability. This section delves into the discomfort that comes with acknowledging patterns that may not be true to one's authentic self. Accepting vulnerability becomes an act of courage, which is required to overcome the fear of judgment and external criticism.

Understanding the Manifestations

To fully comprehend the people-pleasing pattern, it is critical to comprehend its many manifestations. This section digs at how people-pleasing can emerge in several facets of life, such as relationships and decision-making.

In Relationships

Investigate how the people-pleasing habit frequently manifests itself in interpersonal relationships. Understanding these interactions is vital for acceptance and eventual modification, whether it's deferring to others' preferences, avoiding conflict, or prioritizing others' needs above one's own.

Decision-Making Processes

Investigate the impact of people-pleasing on decision-making processes. This section of the chapter asks readers to consider if their choices are motivated by genuine aspirations or the desire to win acceptance. Understanding the impact on decision-making sheds light on the pattern's pervasiveness.

Self-Worth and Validation

Examine how self-worth and validation are linked to people-pleasing habits. Understanding if external validation has become a key source of self-worth and how this dynamic perpetuates the habit is central to our investigation. Recognizing these links is critical for breaking free.

Overcoming Denial and Resistance

Acknowledgement is frequently met with resistance and denial. This section covers common roadblocks that people face when confronted with the people-pleasing pattern.

Strategies for overcoming denial and resistance are investigated, to cultivate a mindset open to transformation and personal progress.

Breaking through Cognitive Dissonance

Cognitive dissonance, or the discomfort of maintaining contradictory thoughts or attitudes, can obstruct recognition. This section of the chapter discusses how to overcome cognitive dissonance, allowing individuals to match their consciousness with their real objectives.

Embracing Non-Judgmental Awareness

Overcoming denial necessitates an objective awareness of one's patterns. Self-reflection should be approached with kindness and curiosity rather than harsh judgment. Accepting nonjudgmental awareness fosters an environment suitable for acknowledgment.

Seeking External Perspectives

External perspectives can sometimes provide useful insights. Seeking feedback from trusted friends, mentors, or professionals who can provide objective observations is part of this method. External viewpoints act as mirrors, reflecting patterns that may be difficult to discern on one's own.

Initiating Self-Compassion

Acknowledgement is linked to self-compassion—a sympathy toward oneself despite recognizing less-than-ideal patterns. This section examines the importance of self-compassion in the acknowledgment process, emphasizing that being flawed is okay and that admission is the first step toward good transformation.

Embracing Imperfections

Accepting flaws is a component of self-compassion. This section of the chapter helps people let go of the expectation of perfection, knowing that admission is a daring step on the path to authenticity. Accepting flaws becomes a freeing component of the acknowledging process.

Cultivating a Growth Mindset

Recognize the possibility of growth and transformation by fostering a growth mindset. This section encourages people to see acknowledgment as a dynamic process—a step toward personal development and living a more honest and happy life.

Building Resilience through Acknowledgment

The process of acknowledgment is not without difficulties. Building resilience is an important part of overcoming the discomfort and probable setbacks that come with admission. This section of the chapter discusses ways to promote resilience and ensure that people stay on the path to liberty.

Individuals get access to the transformational potential of acknowledgment as it becomes a conscious and continuing practice. This section looks at the ramifications of acknowledgment of numerous elements of life, relationships, and human development.

Liberation through Self-Awareness

Recognize the liberating power of self-awareness. This section of the chapter goes into how acknowledgment prepares people for increased self-awareness, helping them to make decisions that are true to themselves.

Strengthening Interpersonal Connections

The transformative journey of awareness includes interpersonal relationships. Relationships improve as people become more in tune with their true desires and boundaries. This section looks at how acknowledgment promotes true interactions based on mutual respect and understanding.

Decision-Making Empowerment

Explore the empowerment that emerges in decision-making. Because acknowledgment frees people from the clutches of external validation, decision-making becomes a purposeful and empowered process. This section of the chapter assists individuals in making decisions that are consistent with their values and objectives.

Creating an Authentic Culture

Acknowledgement has the power to affect larger societal dynamics. This section investigates how individuals can contribute to the formation of a culture that values authenticity, encourages vulnerability, and celebrates the individuality of each individual by accepting acknowledgment.

Chapter Seven exemplifies the important importance of recognizing the people-pleasing habit. Individuals who embrace vulnerability, participate in introspective self-inquiry, and comprehend the pattern's expressions begin a process of self-discovery and empowerment. The subsequent parts will continue to assist individuals through the transformative process of letting go of people-pleasing, paving the way for true life and a freed sense of self.

Self-Empowerment Techniques

As Chapter seven progresses, we enter a vital part of our inquiry: an assessment of actionable solutions for self-empowerment. As the chapter concludes, these tactics become actual instruments that individuals can use in their transformative journey away from the restrictions of people-pleasing. This section emphasizes the critical role that self-empowerment plays not only in breaking away from external validation but also in fostering resilience and agency to align behaviors with one's real self.

Initiating Self-Compassion

The beginning of self-compassion is at the heart of self-empowerment. Acknowledgement and self-compassion intersect, creating a caring environment for people to be kind to themselves even when they recognize less-than-ideal tendencies. This section looks into the critical role of self-compassion in the empowerment process, highlighting the importance of accepting flaws as a first step toward positive change.

Embracing Imperfections

The acceptance of flaws is important to self-compassion. This section of the chapter helps people let go of the heavy expectation of perfection, knowing that admission is a bold step on the path to authenticity. Accepting flaws becomes a freeing aspect of the empowerment process, allowing people to let go of false expectations and cultivate a caring relationship with themselves.

Cultivating a Growth Mindset

Cultivating a growth mentality is a key component of self-empowerment. Recognizing the possibility of growth and change entails perceiving the process as dynamic—a step toward personal development and the cultivation of a more authentic and happy existence. This section offers practical advice on how to cultivate a mindset that views problems as opportunities for growth and learning, allowing individuals to negotiate their journey with perseverance and optimism.

Building Resilience through Acknowledgment

Resilience emerges as an important aspect of self-empowerment. The process of acknowledgment is not without difficulties, and tenacity becomes the bedrock that ensures individuals persevere on the path to liberty. Strategies for developing resilience are examined, including the ability to recover from setbacks, navigate discomfort, and retain momentum in the face of adversity. Building resilience becomes a transforming part of self-empowerment, allowing people to handle the difficulties of their evolving journey.

Embracing the Transformative Power of Acknowledgment

As self-empowerment grows, people discover the transformational power of acknowledgment. This section investigates the ramifications of acknowledgment of numerous aspects of life, relationships, and human development.

Liberation through Self-Awareness

As a result of acceptance, self-awareness grows, acting as a catalyst for release. This section of the chapter goes into how acknowledgment prepares people for increased self-awareness, helping them to make decisions that are true to themselves. Self-awareness becomes a source of empowerment, guiding people toward a more purposeful and fulfilling existence.

Strengthening Interpersonal Connections

The journey of empowerment includes interpersonal connections. Relationships improve as people become more in tune with their true desires and boundaries. This section investigates how self-empowerment promotes true interactions based on mutual respect and understanding. Individuals who are empowered contribute to the development of healthier and more rewarding relationships, having a beneficial ripple effect in their social spheres.

Empowerment in Decision-Making

Through acknowledgment, decision-making becomes an empowered process. Individuals get the courage to make choices that are consistent with their values and objectives once they are free of the grasp of external validation. This section of the chapter helps people navigate decision-making with a fresh sense of empowerment, leading to more intentional and rewarding life paths. Empowered decision-making becomes a pillar of real living.

Nurturing a Culture of Authenticity

Self-aware individuals have a critical role in influencing larger societal processes. This section looks at how individuals can contribute to the formation of a culture that values authenticity, encourages vulnerability, and celebrates the uniqueness of each individual via acknowledgment and empowerment. The empowered individual acts as a catalyst for good cultural shifts, creating an environment that encourages personal development and authenticity.

This chapter finishes by emphasizing the transformative potential of self-empowerment tactics. Individuals who practice self-compassion, establish a growth mindset, strengthen their resilience, and discover the power of acknowledgment pave the path for a more authentic and powerful living. This journey toward self-empowerment serves as the foundation for the ensuing chapters, which each explores distinct aspects of authentic life, resilience, and the never-ending search for personal improvement.

CHAPTER EIGHT

Cultivating Authenticity

As we turn the pages to Chapter Eight, our attention is drawn to the important journey of creating authenticity. This chapter acts as a compass, showing tendencies of people-pleasing while also actively fostering an authentic self. Authenticity is the deliberate alignment of one's actions, values, and choices with one's genuine self. The path begins with the realization that genuine fulfillment comes from being honest to oneself, regardless of external expectations.

Embracing True Self

The fundamental act of embracing one's genuine self is at the heart of authenticity. This part digs into the essence of authenticity, encouraging people to examine their ideas, values, and objectives. The path to authenticity begins with recognizing and celebrating the uniqueness that characterizes each individual. Embracing one's genuine self becomes a freeing gesture, marking a shift away from the people-pleasing façade and toward an authentic expression of individuality.

The Exploration of Core Values

Authenticity is inextricably linked with one's underlying ideals. This section of the chapter leads readers through an exploration of their basic beliefs, provoking thoughts on what is important to them. Identifying and accepting these values acts as a guidepost, directing individuals toward decisions and actions that are consistent with their true selves.

Unveiling Personal Passions

Pursuing own passions is also linked to authenticity. This section encourages people to reveal their unique interests and hobbies, which foster a sense of purpose and fulfillment. Uncovering personal passions helps an individual's real-life story, leading them toward pursuits that provide genuine joy and satisfaction.

Embracing Vulnerability in Authenticity

The path to authenticity necessitates a willingness to embrace vulnerability. This element investigates the relationship between authenticity and vulnerability, highlighting that true authenticity entails being open and honest, even when it is difficult. Embracing vulnerability may be a source of strength, allowing for stronger connections with oneself and others.

Building Confidence outside Approval

Building confidence independent of external approbation is an important aspect of establishing authenticity. This section dives into the dangers of constantly seeking affirmation and approval from others. The path to authenticity is building a strong feeling of self-worth and confidence that is not dependent on outside perceptions.

Detaching from External Validation

Individuals are led through the process of distancing themselves from the need for frequent external approval. This entails accepting that true confidence comes from inside and is not dependent on the views or acceptance of others. Removing oneself from external approval is a freeing step toward authenticity.

Nurturing Intrinsic Confidence

Building confidence without external approbation necessitates cultivating innate confidence. This section of the chapter offers practical ways for growing self-assurance from within by drawing on one's strengths, accomplishments, and personal development. Developing intrinsic confidence provides a long-term foundation for true living.

Embracing Imperfection as Authenticity

Authenticity grows when flaws are acknowledged. This section encourages people to accept their flaws as essential components of their true identities. Recognizing that perfection is an unattainable goal encourages people to develop a sense of self-acceptance and genuine confidence.

Living Authentically in Daily Actions

Authenticity goes beyond self-reflection and displays itself in daily actions and encounters. This section looks at ways people can bring more authenticity into their everyday lives, from communication and decision-making to relationships and work.

Authentic Communication

Communication is how authenticity is expressed. The value of authentic communication—being honest, transparent, and true to oneself in conversations—is discussed in this section of the chapter. Authentic communication develops genuine connections and ensures that one's speech is an accurate reflection of one's ideas and feelings.

Authentic Decision-Making

Authentic life entails making decisions that are in line with one's true self. This section helps individuals approach decision-making with authenticity, taking into account personal values and objectives. Making genuine decisions leads to a more fulfilling and purpose-driven life.

Authentic Relationships

Relationships benefit from cultivating genuineness. Being real, expressing true sentiments, and creating boundaries that match with one's values all contribute to relationship authenticity. This section delves into the complexities of establishing and maintaining genuine connections with others.

Chapter eight lays the groundwork for a journey of transformation toward authenticity. Individuals establish the stage for a life of genuine fulfillment by accepting their true selves, discovering essential beliefs and hobbies, and developing confidence independent of external approval. The following sections will delve deeper into the complexity of authentic life, offering insights and solutions for navigating the challenges of this liberating path.

Embracing True Self

The transforming process of realizing one's self is important to authentic life. The adventure is more than just acknowledging one's individuality; it is a profound exploration that invites people to go into the depths of their existence. It's an invitation to recognize, celebrate, and truly express one's underlying values, beliefs, and objectives.

Core Values Exploration: Navigating the Inner Compass

Embracing one's genuine self begins with a careful examination of one's primary principles. These values, which are frequently the foundation of personal identity, govern decision-making, form relationships, and define an individual's essence. Individuals are invited to unearth the ideas that resonate with their genuine selves through introspection and reflection. This introspective journey is analogous to navigating an inner compass, helping individuals to match their behaviors and decisions with deeply held ideals.

Understanding fundamental values entails a dynamic inquiry into what truly matters, resulting in a road map for living an authentic and purpose-driven life. Individuals who embrace and incorporate these ideals into their daily lives experience a tremendous change toward a more meaningful and fulfilling way of life.

Unveiling Personal Passions: Rediscovering Joy

The pursuit of own passions is intertwined with authentic life. Uncovering these interests is similar to going on a voyage of self-discovery, where layers of interests and desires unique to each individual are gradually unveiled. This section invites people to explore their inner worlds, rediscovering activities that bring them genuine joy and contentment.

Unveiling personal passions is more than just a list of hobbies; it is an investigation into what offers actual contentment and purpose. Whether it's a creative endeavor, a cause, or a lifetime hobby, pursuing personal passions becomes an essential component of living authentically. It motivates people toward a life that is not governed by external expectations, but rather by an innate motivation centered on the pursuit of what truly resonates with their authentic selves.

Embracing Vulnerability in Authenticity: The Strength in Openness

A fearless embrace of vulnerability is required on the path to authenticity. Authentic life does not live behind a mask of invulnerability; rather, it thrives in the true acceptance of one's vulnerabilities. This part goes into the significant relationship between authenticity and vulnerability, highlighting that the true self develops when people dare to be open and honest, even when it is uncomfortable.

Embracing vulnerability may be a source of strength, allowing for stronger connections with oneself and others. It entails tearing down the barriers that keep one's actual self-hidden and allowing the sincere expression of one's thoughts, emotions, and aspirations. Individuals find release in this vulnerability—an unburdening of the urge to comply with societal norms, clearing the way for a more authentic and connected existence.

Embracing one's self is not a one-time event, but rather a lifelong journey of self-discovery and expression. It is a transformative journey that invites individuals to delve into the essence of their being, going beyond the surface-level identity. This comprehensive exploration lays the groundwork for the subsequent sections of Chapter Eight , where the emphasis changes to developing confidence without the need for external approval. Individuals who negotiate the complex terrain of authentic living discover that the actual self is a dynamic and growing entity that is always shaping and reshaping the narrative of a meaningful and fulfilled life.

Building Confidence outside Approval

As we delve into the delicate process of establishing confidence independent of external acceptance, our journey towards authenticity takes a revolutionary turn. This part acts as a compass, steering people away from the temptations of always seeking validation and approval from others. Building confidence outside of acceptance is a critical component of growing authenticity, requiring a strong sense of self-worth that isn't dependent on outside perceptions.

Detaching from External Validation

The conscious act of separating from the need for frequent external validation is a critical step in gaining confidence outside approval. This necessitates a radical adjustment in perspective—acceptance that true confidence comes from inside and is not dependent on the views or approval of others. Detaching from external validation is a liberating step toward authenticity, releasing people from the shackles of seeking validation in every action or decision.

Individuals might anchor their confidence in an internal reservoir of self-assurance by realizing that external validation is transient and often subjective. This internal affirmation grows into a durable and empowering source, allowing people to navigate life's complexity with authenticity and resilience.

Nurturing Intrinsic Confidence

Building confidence without external approbation necessitates the development of internal confidence. This section offers practical ways for developing self-assurance from the inside by focusing on one's qualities, accomplishments, and personal development. Nurturing intrinsic confidence entails a conscious effort to recognize and celebrate one's strengths, accomplishments, and the road to ongoing self-improvement.

Individuals are urged to cultivate a positive internal dialogue in which they acknowledge their strengths and embrace a worldview that values personal worth irrespective of external evaluations. Individuals become less subject to the vagaries of external opinions as intrinsic confidence grows, producing a solid and resilient sense of self.

Embracing Imperfection as Authenticity

Accepting faults as authentic is a key component of developing confidence outside of approval. This part urges people to see that authenticity blooms in the acceptance of flaws. The goal of perfection is replaced by accepting oneself, imperfections and all, as an essential component of one's real self.

Accepting flaws becomes a significant act of self-acceptance, freeing individuals from the unreasonable expectations set by cultural conventions. It enables people to create an honest sense of self-worth, appreciate the uniqueness of their experience, and find strength in vulnerability.

Living Authentically in Daily Actions

Individuals are set to pour authenticity into their daily lives with greater confidence independent of external approbation. This section looks at how authenticity presents itself in daily actions and interactions, and how it influences communication, decision-making, relationships, and work.

Authentic Communication

Authentic communication expresses authentic living vividly. This section of the chapter discusses the significance of speaking with honesty, openness, and an authentic representation of one's actual self. Authentic communication encourages true connections, guarantees that one's voice is an accurate portrayal of one's thoughts and feelings, and helps to a more meaningful exchange of ideas.

Authentic Decision-Making

Authentic life extends to decision-making, in which people approach choices with their true selves in mind. This section assists individuals in making honest decisions while considering personal beliefs and objectives. Individuals make decisions that reflect their real personality, which leads to a more fulfilling and purpose-driven life.

Authentic Relationships

Being real, expressing true sentiments, and creating boundaries that match with one's values all contribute to cultivating authenticity in relationships. This section delves into the complexities of establishing and maintaining genuine connections with others. Mutual respect, understanding, and appreciation for each other's actual selves characterize authentic relationships.

As Chapter eight concludes, the transforming journey of cultivating authenticity is centered on developing confidence in the absence of external approbation. Individuals are liberated from the restrictions of needing constant acceptance by detaching from external validation, fostering internal confidence, and embracing faults. This newfound confidence allows individuals to live truly in their daily actions, cultivating genuine friendships, and making decisions that are true to themselves.

This chapter's conclusion is a critical turning point on the path to authenticity. Individuals who manage the subtle interplay of accepting their actual selves and growing confidence outside of approval establish the framework for the following chapters, which delve deeper into the nuances of authentic living.

CHAPTER NINE

Nurturing Well-Being: Emotional and Mental Health

As we embark on Chapter Nine, the emphasis switches to the essential topic of nurturing emotional and mental well-being. This chapter looks into the fundamentals of emotional and mental health, emphasizing the importance of these aspects in the journey of authentic life. This inquiry includes not only the need of prioritizing self-care but also the acknowledgment of when professional help is required. This chapter emphasizes the complex relationship between well-being and authenticity, recognizing that a healthy mind and heart provide the groundwork for a truly fulfilling existence.

Prioritizing Self-Care: A Foundation for Well-Being

Prioritizing self-care is a fundamental strategy for supporting emotional and mental well-being. This section delves into the subtle components of self-care, going beyond the standard definition to include behaviors that promote a harmonic balance between an individual's physical, emotional, and mental aspects.

Holistic Self-Care Practices

Adopting holistic techniques that respond to the multidimensional character of well-being is part of prioritizing self-care. This section of the chapter discusses the significance of embracing habits that nourish the body, mind, and spirit. Holistic self-care becomes a cornerstone for emotional and mental wellness, ranging from physical activities and proper eating to mindfulness and relaxation techniques.

Emotional Resilience through Self-Care

Self-care is more than just treating oneself; it is a conscious investment in one's emotional resilience. This section looks at how self-care activities contribute to emotional strength, giving people the tools they need to deal with life's challenges, disappointments, and inescapable stressors. Emotional resilience develops as a result of continuous and intentional self-care.

The Role of Boundaries in Self-Care

Boundaries are important in self-care because they define the limits of what is acceptable and respectful in numerous parts of life. This section discusses the need to create and maintain healthy boundaries to protect one's emotional and mental well-being. Setting limits becomes an empowering tool for those who want to live authentically without jeopardizing their mental health.

While self-care is an important foundation, there are times when professional help is required. This section navigates the subtleties of detecting when external aid is required and investigates the many paths for requesting assistance.

The Stigma Surrounding Mental Health

Before getting professional help, it is critical to overcome the stigma associated with mental health. This section of the chapter dispels cultural myths, encouraging people to regard getting help as a courageous and responsible act rather than a show of weakness. Individuals are more likely to seek professional help for mental health issues if mental health issues are de-stigmatized.

Recognizing the Signs

Recognizing when to seek professional help entails being aware of the symptoms of emotional and mental discomfort. This section contains information on common indicators that may indicate the need for outside assistance. Recognizing these indications, which range from persistent sorrow and worry to disturbances in daily functioning, encourages individuals to take proactive steps to address their well-being.

Avenues for Professional Support

Seeking professional help can take many forms, ranging from therapy and counseling to psychiatric intervention. This section investigates the various possibilities available, emphasizing the significance of selecting the best fit for individual needs. It elucidates the transforming power of professional help in offering tools, insights, and coping mechanisms for facing life's obstacles.

Chapter nine lays the foundation for an in-depth examination of the relationship between well-being and authentic life. Individuals lay the way for a life distinguished by emotional and mental resilience by prioritizing self-care and understanding the significance of obtaining professional help when needed. The next parts will explore deeper into the complexities of cultivating well-being and its symbiotic relationship with authenticity.

Prioritizing Self-Care

As Chapter Nine progresses, the emphasis shifts to the underlying pillar of well-being: prioritizing self-care. This section delves deeply into the various facets of self-care, going beyond the usual definition to include practices that promote harmony in the physical, emotional, and mental domains. The principle is straightforward: a strong commitment to self-care is not a luxury but an essential investment in one's emotional and mental health.

Holistic Self-Care Practices: Nourishing Body, Mind, and Soul

Prioritizing self-care begins with adopting holistic practices that address the multidimensional character of well-being. This part discusses the significance of including activities that nourish the body, mind, and spirit. Holistic self-care becomes a cornerstone for fostering emotional and mental wellness, from regular physical activity and a balanced eating plan to including mindfulness and relaxation practices.

In the pursuit of happiness, the body and mind are inextricably linked, and neglecting one can have an impact on the other. Holistic self-care approaches acknowledge this deep link, ensuring that people treat their physical health, emotional balance, and mental clarity all at the same time. Individuals who take a holistic approach establish the foundations for a sturdy foundation that supports their real journey.

Emotional Resilience through Self-Care: Building Inner Strength

Beyond the superficial notion of self-care as a form of indulgence, it is a conscious investment in emotional resiliency. This section investigates how consistent and intentional self-care routines lead to emotional fortification. Individuals armed with emotional resilience endure life's obstacles, disappointments, and stressors with grace and adaptation.

Self-care becomes a toolkit for emotion management, giving individuals coping methods for dealing with stress, anxiety, and the challenges of daily life. Individuals who create emotional resilience via self-care not only maintain their mental health but also cultivate a sense of inner power that motivates them toward authentic life.

The Role of Boundaries in Self-Care: Safeguarding Emotional and Mental Well-Being

The construction and maintenance of appropriate boundaries are essential to self-care. This section dives into the critical function that boundaries play in ensuring emotional and mental well-being. Setting limits becomes an empowering tool for those who want to live authentically without jeopardizing their mental health.

Healthy boundaries define what is appropriate and respectful in numerous parts of life, including personal, professional, and social interactions. Individuals defend themselves against emotional tiredness, burnout, and the negative repercussions of overextending by explicitly establishing these limitations. Setting boundaries to prioritize self-care is an act of self-respect that conserves the energy required for true life.

The transforming path of prioritizing self-care as the cornerstone of emotional and mental well-being is explored in Chapter Nine. Individuals can navigate the complex terrain of authentic living by embracing holistic practices, developing emotional resilience, and establishing healthy boundaries.

The chapter's conclusion is a watershed moment in realizing that self-care is not a luxury reserved for a select few, but rather an essential requirement for everyone on the path to authenticity.

Seeking Professional Support

The chapter finishes by providing light on the critical topic of obtaining professional help in the intricate fabric of emotional and mental well-being. Recognizing when to seek outside help is a critical step toward cultivating a resilient and authentic inner landscape. This part delves into the intricacies of recognizing indications of distress, addressing the stigma associated with mental health, and navigating the various professional assistance options available.

The Stigma Surrounding Mental Health

Before getting into the complexities of seeking professional help, it is critical to address the prevalent stigma associated with mental health. This section of the chapter dispels cultural myths, encouraging people to regard getting help as a courageous and responsible act rather than a show of weakness. Individuals are more likely to seek professional help for mental health issues if mental health issues are de-stigmatized.

The stigma frequently works as a barrier, preventing people from identifying and resolving their emotional and mental health issues. Dispelling these myths fosters an environment in which requesting help is not only accepted but also applauded as a proactive move toward well-being and authenticity.

Recognizing the Signs

Recognizing when to seek professional help requires being aware of the indicators of emotional and mental suffering. This section contains information on common indicators that may indicate the need for outside assistance. Recognizing these indications, which range from persistent sorrow and worry to disturbances in daily functioning, encourages individuals to take proactive steps to address their well-being.

The story stresses the significance of self-awareness and reflection. Individuals can notice departures from their baseline well-being and take timely action by analyzing their emotional landscape. Recognizing the indications becomes a compass that directs people toward the help they require for a happier and more authentic existence.

Avenues for Professional Support

Seeking professional assistance includes several options, each adapted to particular needs and interests. This section delves into the range of alternatives accessible, from therapeutic interventions and counseling to psychiatric consultation. The chapter emphasizes that the path to healing is not one-size-fits-all, and individuals are urged to investigate and find the support system that is right for them.

Psychotherapy and counseling provide a secure environment for people to examine and navigate their emotions. Different approaches to self-discovery and healing, such as cognitive-behavioral therapy (CBT) or mindfulness-based approaches are available.

Psychiatric Intervention: When medicine is required, psychiatric support becomes an essential component of the professional assistance available. Therapists and psychiatrists work together to ensure a complete approach to mental health.

Support Groups: Peer support can be a vital component of professional assistance. Participating in support groups encourages people to connect with others who are going through similar things, establishing a sense of community and understanding.

As Chapter nine concludes, the study of well-being includes both self-care and seeking professional help. Individuals lay the groundwork for a holistic approach to well-being by detecting indicators of distress, confronting the stigma around mental health, and embracing many options for aid.

The chapter emphasizes that seeking professional help is not a sign of weakness, but rather a brave step toward a healthier, more honest existence. Self-care and professional support work together to form a strong framework for individuals to manage the complexities of their emotional and mental terrain.

CONCLUSION

Reflections on Progress

In the culmination of this transformative journey, we find ourselves at a juncture of introspection and reflection. Learning to quit pleasing everyone has been a remarkable voyage that has revealed levels of self-discovery, perseverance, and authenticity. The nature of this activity becomes clearer when we reflect on the progress achieved, the insights obtained, and the paths forked.

Unveiling the Complexity of People-Pleasing

The investigation began by defining and unraveling the layers of people-pleasing, recognizing its attractiveness as well as the social processes that lead to its persistence. We investigated the traits of a people-pleaser and identified the warning indicators that often go unreported. Understanding the various layers of motive behind people-pleasing provided a more nuanced perspective, exposing how it infiltrates our lives in subtle ways.

The Cost of People-Pleasing

We faced the price of people-pleasing as our journey progressed—emotional toll, mental effort, and the eroding of appropriate boundaries. We investigated the difficult balance between saying "no" without feeling guilty and the unintended repercussions of continuously favoring others over oneself. We discovered the significant costs hidden in the fabric of people-pleasing by peeling back the layers of motivation.

Embracing Authentic Living

The focus of the story then changed to liberation from people-pleasing, emphasizing the significance of developing personal values and matching actions with underlying convictions. Individuals learned to embrace their genuine selves after breaking free from the shackles of external affirmation, building resilience and strength. The pursuit of authenticity becomes a guiding light, illuminating the route to a life founded on honest expression and self-empowerment.

Nurturing Well-Being

Recognizing the deep relationship between honesty and well-being, the investigation expanded to prioritize self-care and seek expert help. The chapter underlined the need to foster emotional and mental wellness as part of the authentic journey. Individuals maintained their well-being by learning when to seek help and embracing various forms of support, laying the framework for a meaningful and resilient existence.

Key Takeaways and Moving Forward

Saying "no" without feeling guilty is a powerful statement of personal limits.

Authentic life necessitates a deliberate alignment of behaviors with basic ideals.

Well-being is a constant discipline that necessitates self-care and, when necessary, professional assistance.

The journey to stop pleasing everyone is a dynamic process, not a fixed destination.

One

Moving Forward

As we move forward, let these key takeaways be beacons guiding our path:

Accept Imperfection: Genuine life accepts defects as a part of the human experience. Accept them as the threads that weave the tapestry of authenticity.

Cultivate Boundaries: Creating and maintaining healthy boundaries is a continuous process. It's an act of self-respect and a key component of living genuinely.

Prioritize Self-Care: Self-care is a necessity, not an indulgence. To maintain the resilience required for true life, prioritize activities that nourish your body, mind, and spirit.

Seek Help: Recognize when outside assistance is required. Seeking professional assistance is a brave step toward happiness and an investment in an honest life.

Let the lessons learned resonate in our decisions, reverberate in our actions, and drive us toward a life lived truly as we end this inquiry on learning to quit pleasing everyone. The adventure does not end here; it continues to evolve. May the chapters published serve as a source of inspiration, empowerment, and resilience as we journey down the winding road of authenticity. Every stride forward is a validation of our dedication to being true to ourselves—a commitment that opens the way for a life full of meaning, connection, and the unflinching confidence to live authentically.